# Remembering

# REMEMBERING

Niagara

## TALES FROM BEYOND THE FALLS

BOB KOSTOFF

THE
History
PRESS

Published by The History Press
Charleston, SC 29403
www.historypress.net

First published 2008

Manufactured in the United Kingdom

ISBN 978.1.59629.451.6

Library of Congress Cataloging-in-Publication Data

Kostoff, Robert D.
Remembering Niagara : tales from beyond the falls / Robert D. Kostoff.
p. cm.
Includes bibliographical references.
ISBN 978-1-59629-451-6
1. Niagara (N.Y. : Town)--History--Anecdotes. 2. Niagara (N.Y. : Town)--Biography--
Anecdotes. 3. Niagara Falls Region (N.Y. and Ont.)--History--Anecdotes. I. Title.
F129.N78K67 2008
974.7'98--dc22
2007052985

*To*
*Nephews Jimmy, Stevie and Chuckie Pettitt*
*and Niece Linda Stover*

# Contents

# Contents

# Preface

It is generally helpful for people to know where they have been in order to figure out where they are going. In this sense, history melds into the future. Therefore, no one can credibly say that the study of history is unimportant.

One of the most interesting historical places in the United States is Niagara County in western New York State, not only because it contains the world famous Niagara Falls, but also because it has been home to many exciting inhabitants. These are the people about whom I write and whom I have come to admire, as I am sure you will too as you read this book.

In addition to the city of Niagara Falls, Niagara County contains the cities of Lockport, the county seat, and North Tonawanda. The county contains 532 square miles between Lakes Erie and Ontario, and the population exceeds 225,000 souls.

I have been researching and writing local history for more years than I care to remember. As a lifelong journalist, I have written local history feature stories for the *Niagara Gazette*, *Buffalo Courier-Express* and the *Lockport Journal*. For the last several years, I have written a local history column in the weekly *Niagara Falls Reporter*. The stories in this book, by and large, have appeared in the *Reporter*. I want to thank Publisher Bruce Battaglia and Editor-in-Chief Mike Hudson for their support of this book.

*Remembering Niagara: Tales from Beyond the Falls* is a sequel to my book *Nuggets of Niagara County History.*

# PART I

# Native Americans

# The Neuter Nation

One of the most incisive accounts of the Neuter Indians came in a seventeenth-century letter from Jesuit missionary Father Gabriel L'Allemant to the Jesuit provincial in France. The Neuter, or Neutral Indians, occupied the Niagara Region on both sides of the Niagara River in the seventeenth century. Early French fur traders called them Neuter because they kept a neutral territory between the warring Hurons in Canada and Senecas to the east.

Father L'Allemant's report was dated May 19, 1641. It was sent from the Jesuit Mission of Saint Mary's located in Canada near Lake Huron. He wrote of the trip of two other Jesuits, Jean Brebeuf and Joseph Chaumonot, to the Neuter nation. The Senecas later tortured to death both Fathers L'Allemant and Brebeuf.

Concerning the Neuters, L'Allemant's letter stated, "Father Brebeuf is particularly fitted for such an expedition, God having in an eminent degree endowed him with a capacity for learning languages." While many French traders had visited the area "to profit by their furs and other commodities," L'Allemant reported that "few missionaries visited there."

The only previous preaching of the Catholic gospel, he wrote, was by "Father De La Roch Daillon, a Recollect, who passed the winter there in the year 1626." It was a four- or five-day journey from the land of the Huron to the Neuter Nation.

The explorers estimated that there were about forty villages of Neuters, all but three or four of them on the western, or Canadian, side of the Niagara River. They described the Great Lakes' drainage pattern as flowing "into the lake of Erie, or the Nation of the Cat, from thence it enters the territory of the Neuter nation and takes the name of Onghiaahra [Niagara] until it empties into Ontario, or St. Louis Lake."

Regarding the Neuter population, L'Allemant wrote that, "according to the estimate of these illustrious fathers who have been there, the Neuter Nation comprises about 12,000 souls, which enables them to furnish 4,000 warriors."

L'Allemant believed the Neuter name was aptly applied because "their country being the ordinary passage by land between some of the Iroquois nations and the Hurons, who are sworn enemies, they remained at peace with both."

About the origin of the Native Americans, L'Allemant wrote:

> *There is every reason for believing that not long since the Hurons, Iroquois and Neuter Nations formed one people and originally came from the same family, but have in the lapse of time became separated from each other, more or less in distance, interests and affection so that some are now enemies, others neutral and others still live in intimate friendship and intercourse.*

He said their food was similar to that of the Hurons and consisted of corn, beans and gourds, fish and game, including deer, buffaloes, wildcats, wolves, wild boars, beavers and wild turkeys. Hunting was good that year, he said, because of a heavy snow. "It is rare," he wrote, "to see snow in this country more than half a foot deep. But this year it is more than three feet."

He described their dress thus:

> *The men, like all savages, cover their naked flesh with skins but are less particular than the Hurons in concealing what should not appear. The squaws are ordinarily clothed, at least from waist to knees, but are more free and shameless in their immodesty than the Hurons.*

According to L'Allemant, the Neuters differed from the Hurons in that they were "larger, stronger and better formed. They also have more affection for the dead and have a greater number of fools or jugglers."

A day's journey to the east of the Neuters was the Seneca Nation, "most dreaded by the Hurons." Although these missionaries returned safely from the Neuter Nation, the dread of the Seneca proved to be prophetic. A section of *The Jesuit Relations* was titled "A Veritable Account of the Martyrdom and Blessed Death of Father Jean de Brebouf and of Father Gabriel L'Allemant in New France in the Country of the Hurons by the Iroquois, Enemies of the Faith."

The Senecas took the Huron village of Saint Ignace and captured the two priests, "stripped them entirely naked and fastened each to a post."

The horrendous torture, described in detail, included beating them with clubs, ripping out their fingernails, pouring boiling water over them and burning them with red-hot hatchets. During this torture, Father Brebeuf kept preaching about God so that, "to prevent him from speaking more, they cut off his tongue and both his upper and lower lips. After that they set themselves to strip the flesh from his legs, thighs and arms, to the very bone, and then put it to roast before his eyes in order to eat it."

A mosaic portrait of Saint Jean Brebeuf is among the lineup of saints and prospective saints above the pews in Saint Mary of the Cataract Church, the mother church of Niagara Falls, New York. Some believe that Father Brebeuf had a beatific vision of a huge cross and that he saw it in the mist of the falls.

Eighteenth-century French Jesuit explorer and historian Pierre Charlevoix described the fate of the Neuter Nation. He wrote:

> *A people larger, stronger and better formed than any other savages and who lived south of the Huron country were visited by the Jesuits who preached to them the Kingdom of God.*
>
> *They were called the Neuter Nation because they took no part in the wars which desolated the country. But in the end, they could not themselves escape entire destruction.*
>
> *To avoid the fury of the Iroquois, they finally joined them against the Hurons, but gained nothing by the union. The Iroquois, that like lions that have tasted blood, cannot be satiated, destroyed indiscriminately all that came in their way, and at this day there remains no trace of the Neuter Nation.*

# Father Brebeuf's Vision

Not only did the Native Americans believe that the awesome falls of Niagara had mystical powers, but some Europeans also believed that they were the source of a miraculous vision for an early Catholic missionary. This is the story of Father Jean Brebeuf, a Jesuit priest, who, along with his confrere Father Joseph Chaumonot, traveled to Niagara

A mosaic of the seal of Niagara County in the rotunda floor of the Niagara County Courthouse in Lockport, New York.

in 1640 to convert the Neuter Nation of Indians to Catholicism. This particular tale was contained in some 1928 articles by the Old Fort Niagara Association, Inc., designed to "enable students of the local schools to prepare and submit essays on the ideals of the pioneers of the 17th century."

The two priests journeyed to Niagara through Canada from the Huron Indian Territory. While they generally proceeded safely through Indian lands, their intentions were suspect. Rumors among Native Americans spread that the priests were magicians who carried "all manner of evils with them." Therefore, the reception of the missionaries by the Neuter Indians was not the most cordial. The two arrived in the area of what is now Queenston in Canada and then crossed the river to the Neuter village of Ongiara at present-day Lewiston.

The priests set up an altar and assured the Indians they were on a mission of peace and goodwill. They only wanted to tell the Indians about the Christian God. The Neuters, however, were having none of the white man's religion.

Apparently realizing discretion was the better part of valor, the priests decided in the middle of February 1641 to pack up and head back to the Huron settlement in Canada. Cold, half starved and wading through deep snow, they tramped through the woods until they came to a cluster of bark lodges. Here, they were offered respite. Father Chaumonot went to sleep, but

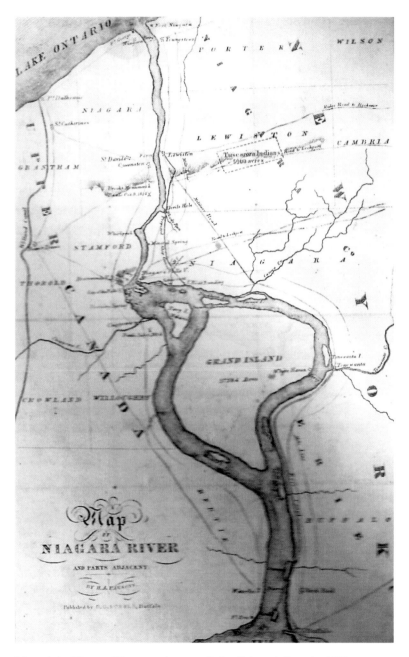

Map of the Niagara River area between Lakes Erie and Ontario, 1850.

A view of the American Falls as seen from Prospect Point.

Father Brebeuf, to escape for a time the acrid and pungent smoke that filled the cabin, went out to commune with God.

It was at this point, as the story is told, that Father Brebeuf had his vision.

> *Far away to the northeast, high in the air and boldly outlined,*
> *a huge cross hung suspended in mid-heaven. It moved toward*
> *him from the land of the Iroquois. The saintly face lighted*
> *with unwonted splendor for he saw the vision which presaged*
> *of a martyr's crown.*

Some people believe that Father Brebeuf had a heavenly vision while staring at the mist from the falls, but at this point in his journey he was near present-day Grimsby, too far from the falls to view the mists. However, as members of the Old Fort Niagara Association noted in 1928, "this story is a remarkable example of the devotion and sincerity of purpose of the first missionary who ever attempted to set up Christianity on the banks of the Niagara."

Saint Jean Brebeuf chronicled some strange tales of Native Americans in rather extensive writings before they killed him. Some of his intriguing letters, which were sent back to France in the 1600s for inclusion in *The Jesuit Relations* book, included details of the beginning of life, the trial of murderers, the famed Indian death dance and the unique Huron language.

The Hurons, like their cousins the Iroquois, have some distinct tales of the beginning of life on earth. One of the most intriguing tales, as told by Brebeuf, claims that, in the beginning, a man, a fox and a "little animal like a marten, were isolated on a small island surrounded by water." The man told the fox to dive into the water to see how deep it was. The fox refused, so the man kicked it into the water, never to see it again. He then told the other animal to dive into the water. The animal did, found it was shallow, hit his snout on the muddy bottom and then returned with the soil.

This encouraged the man and he had the animal keep doing this until the soil expanded the tiny island "into the vast country that we see today." Brebeuf, mainly concerned with converting the Indians, proceeded to ask a series of pointed questions about that first man, such as: "Who gave him life? Who put him upon this little island? How could he become the father of all these nations if he was alone and had no companion?" The only explanation the Hurons could give was: "We do not know. This is what we were told; our fathers never taught us any more about it."

Regarding justice for murder, Brebeuf wrote:

> *The relatives of the deceased not only prosecute the individual who committed the murder but address their complaint to his entire village, which must make restitution. For this purpose, they must provide up to 60 presents as soon as possible, the least of which must be the value of one new beaver robe.*

There was a long, involved ceremony of providing the presents, usually performed by the chief. If, by chance, the relatives exacted revenge by killing the murderer, then they had to compensate the relatives of the murderer.

In "The Solemn Feast of the Dead," written in 1636, Brebeuf described this intricate ceremony that took place about every decade. Relatives exhumed the bodies of all their loved ones and carried them to a central gravesite. "This feast abounds in ceremonies," Brebeuf wrote. He added that the "principal ceremony is that of the kettle" for cooking food.

After the bodies had been dug up, the relatives would "take them from the cemeteries, bear them on their shoulders and cover them with the finest robes they have." He noted, "The flesh of some is quite gone and there is only a sort of parchment on their bones."

The bodies were put on display in a large cabin while feasting and games took place. Then the bodies were taken to a large pit, "about ten feet deep and five fathoms in diameter." When all the bodies were in the pit, filling it to within two feet of the top, they were covered with robes, mats and bark. Then there was more feasting, eating and gift giving.

The language of the Huron, quite different from that of the Iroquois, provided particular difficulty for missionaries because "as they have hardly any virtue or religion, or any learning or government, they have consequently no individual words suitable for signifying these things. Hence it is that we are at a loss in explaining to them many important matters depending upon a knowledge of these things." Brebeuf said that the language had no consonants of B, F, L, M, P, X or Z, and that their talk consisted mainly of vowels.

Brebeuf and his superior, Gabriel L'Allemant, met their ends in 1649 when the Iroquois virtually annihilated the Hurons. Jesuit missionary Paul Ragueneau told this story. About a thousand Iroquois warriors, armed with firearms obtained from the Dutch, "made a difficult journey of nearly 200 leagues over snow in order to take us by surprise."

Brebeuf and L'Allemant were in an area called the mission of Saint Ignace, which consisted of a cluster of five villages. The Iroquois arrived at the first village on March 16, 1649, and attacked so suddenly that they captured the village before a defense could be mounted. Ragueneau wrote, "Only three men escaped, running almost naked across the snows. They bore the alarm and spread the terror to a neighboring town, about a league distant." The enemy captured that town and set it afire. "They cast into the flames," Ragueneau wrote, "the old, the sick, the children who had not been able to escape, and all those being too severely wounded, could not have followed them into captivity."

In that town were Brebeuf and L'Allemant, both of whom some of the converted Huron had urged to flee before the Iroquois attack. They could have easily departed with the five hundred Indians who did leave, but "the zeal could not permit such a thing," Ragueneau wrote.

The two priests were baptizing and giving absolution to the victims as the fight raged around them. According to Ragueneau, "This band of Christians fell mostly alive into the hands of the enemy and with them our two fathers, the pastors of that church." Brebeuf and L'Allemant were horribly tortured, burned and sliced up before they finally perished.

# Travails of Father Jogues

Jesuit missionaries who came to New France in the seventeenth century were often martyred at the hands of Native Americans resentful of the intrusion into their culture. One of these martyrs was Jean Brebeuf. Another confrere of this holy man was Isaac Jogues, who told a rather horrific story about his contact with the Iroquois. The informative letters these men sent back to France, while hardly presenting an objective view, detailed conditions in the New World, and they were compiled in some seventy volumes known as *The Jesuit Relations*.

In one of these missives, L'Allemant said that Jogues was making a journey from the Montreal area to Quebec when the Iroquois captured him. Jogues himself wrote, "And so we set out in danger from the moment of departure." At this time, war existed between the Iroquois in New York and the Huron and Algonquian (French allies) in Canada. Jogues reported that the entourage reached Quebec safely, concluded business in fifteen days and then set out on the return journey on August 1, 1642. He wrote, "The first day was favorable to us, but the second caused us to fall into the hands of the Iroquois."

There were forty people in the retinue, mostly Huron guides. "We were four French," Jogues wrote, "one of whom was at the rear and escaped with the Hurons." Jogues was able to hide among "very tall and dense reeds," but he had second thoughts about abandoning his confreres. He showed himself to an Iroquois guard and was taken captive with the others.

One Frenchman was able to shoot and kill an attacker, but he was then badly beaten by the others. Jogues consoled the wounded man, entreating him to keep the faith. He said the Iroquois perhaps imagined "that [he] was applauding this young man for killing one of their captains and they fell upon [him] with a mad fury." The Iroquois, most likely Mohawk from eastern New York, "stabbed at [Jogues] and beat [him] and overwhelmed [him] with blows from their war clubs, flinging [him] to the ground, half dead." He wrote:

> When I began to catch my breath, the men who had not participated in the beating came up and used their teeth to tear out my fingernails. Then they took turns biting the ends of my two index fingers and with the nail gone, this caused me excruciating pain, as if they were being ground and crushed between two stones until small bone splinters began to protrude.

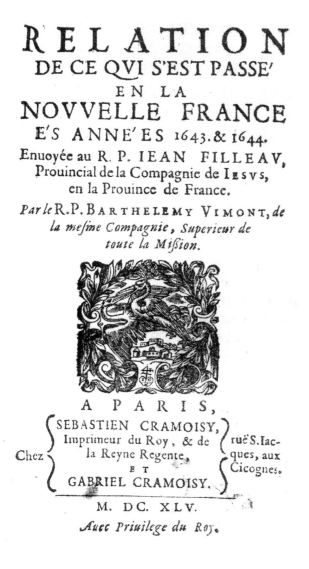

RELATION
DE CE QVI S'EST PASSE'
EN LA
NOVVELLE FRANCE
E'S ANNE'ES 1643.& 1644.
Enuoyée au R. P. IEAN FILLEAV,
Prouincial de la Compagnie de Iᴇsvs,
en la Prouince de France.

*Par le* R.P. BARTHELEMY VIMONT, *de
la mesme Compagnie, Superieur de
toute la Miſsion.*

A PARIS,
Chez { SEBASTIEN CRAMOISY,
Imprimeur du Roy, & de
la Reyne Regente,
ᴇ ᴛ
GABRIEL CRAMOISY. } { rue S.Iac-
ques, aux
Cicognes.

M. DC. XLV.
*Auec Priuilege du Roy.*

The title page of the book *The Jesuit Relations*, published in Paris in 1644 with harrowing accounts of missionary work among Native Americans.

When the torture subsided, Jogues returned to his calling and "went round to all the captives, baptizing those who were not yet baptized, encouraging these poor wretches to suffer steadfastly in the assurance that their reward would far exceed the severity of their torments."

The Iroquois led the twenty-two captives on a thirteen-day journey to their territory, all the while beating and tormenting them. Jogues said the untreated wounds soon "became putrid and worm infested." They soon met up with another war party of two hundred Iroquois, who joined in the entertainment by forming a gauntlet. According to Jogues, there were "a hundred on one side and a hundred on the other and [they] forced us, all naked as we were, to pass in between along that path of fury and anguish."

Jogues wrote that he was knocked to the ground and continually beaten by war clubs until near death. The Iroquois, not wanting to lose a captive, then "tenderly picked [him] up and carried [him] all bleeding to the stage they had prepared." When he came to, they started beating him again "on [his] head, on [his] neck and all over [his] body." Then some "burned one of [his] fingers and crushed another with their teeth. They squeezed and twisted those that were already torn with a demonic rage, they scratched at [his] wounds with their nails and, when strength failed [him], they applied fire to [his] arm and thighs."

They arrived at an Iroquois village. By then Jogues had only two fingernails left "and those barbarians tore them from [him] with their teeth, rending the flesh from beneath and cutting it clean to the bone with their nails which they grow very long." The captives were put through another terrifying gauntlet. Then, almost completely naked, they were made to climb a scaffold in the center of the village. Jogues said one Iroquois ordered a squaw to cut off his thumb and "finally, she had to obey and she cut the thumb from [his] left hand."

They were tied up at night and given over to children who threw hot coals on them. They were led to other villages where the tortures resumed. Then, miraculously, the Indians decided not to kill the captives, apparently to enhance their bargaining position with the French.

Jogues managed to escape and made his way to the Dutch in Albany. He was taken back to France, but he returned to the New World later to resume his mission. Captured again, he was killed by a tomahawk blow to the head.

# Ancient Mounds

One of the most pervasive and intriguing aspects of local history is the theory that a more advanced race of humans existed here even before the Iroquois Indians arrived. The theory stems from the discovery of a series of huge mounds spanning the area from New York State to the Mississippi

Valley. These mounds, according to archeologists, were used as forts and as burial grounds. Uncovered relics indicate that these forts were built by a highly advanced race of non-Indians. But the speculation is confused because, later, Indians also used these mounds and left plenty of their own relics.

The prominent nineteenth-century scholar, statesman and governor DeWitt Clinton, who had traveled over the portage of Niagara, subscribed to such a theory. Clinton, who stayed with Judge Augustus Porter on his trip to Niagara, was governor from 1817–23 and again from 1825–28. Known as the "father of the Erie Canal," Clinton presented a written paper on the subject at a talk before the New York Historical Society in 1811. He began his discourse with the statement that "previous to the occupation of this country by the progenitors of the present race of Indians, it was inhabited by a race of men much more populous and much farther advanced in civilization."

Probably the most popular theory is that humans migrated from the cold of Siberia across the glacier to Alaska and then down the continent into South America. This migration is believed to have occurred about ten thousand years ago. A recent PBS program on the beginnings of humankind traced a human gene through people living today from Africa to middle Europe and up to northern Siberia, bolstering the migration theory.

Clinton said he personally inspected several of the mounds, which were from two to six acres in size in the form of an irregular ellipsis. The earth breastwork was up to eight feet tall. Clinton commented:

> *These fortifications, thus diffused over the interior of our country, have been generally considered as surpassing the skill, patience and industry of the Indian race, and various hypotheses have been advanced to prove them of European origin.*

Some hold to the theory that Europeans came to this country following the Iceland and Greenland route of Leif Ericson, but centuries before Ericson made his trip to the New World.

In Niagara County, these mounds have been discovered on the Tuscarora Reservation in a section once known as Kienuka, on top of the escarpment and in the town of Cambria, near Lockport, between Lewiston and Niagara Falls and on Tonawanda Island in North Tonawanda.

Clinton said that it was clear these forts "were not the work of the Indians" because the Seneca "did not pretend to know anything about them." Also, he said, "the erection of such prodigious works must have been the result of labor far beyond the patience and perseverance of our Indians and the form and materials are entirely different from those which they are known to make." Additionally, Clinton noted that ditches often protected these ancient fortifications. The Indians used palisades for protection and not entrenchments.

The escarpment, according to Clinton, extends seventy-eight miles from Rochester to Lewiston and was once the shoreline of Lake Ontario. All of the mounds discovered, he pointed out, are south of the ridge because in ancient times the lake encompassed the area north of the ridge, indicating that the forts were constructed in antiquity before Lake Ontario receded.

Clinton said this ancient race probably migrated from Asia, but centuries before the present Indians came. He said, "The first stream of people that flowed into America must have remained free from external pressure for ages." In a period of tranquility, these ancient people "would devote themselves to the arts of peace, make rapid progress in civilization and acquire an immense population." But eventually, discord and war broke out and "at last they became alarmed by the eruption of a horde of barbarians who rushed in like an overwhelming flood from the north of Asia." These "barbarians," Clinton conjectured, overran the country and wiped out nearly all signs of the previous civilization, with only the mounds remaining. Later, the Indians used these mounds—archeologists have found arrowheads, clay pipes and many other Iroquois relics, including human bones.

Lockport newspaper editor and historian Orsamus Turner, in his 1850 book *Pioneer History of the Holland Purchase*, wrote that he had viewed one such mound "at the head of a deep gorge a mile west of Lockport." Turner, more than a century and a half ago, pondered over this supposed ancient race. Today, we are not much closer than he was to finding positive proof. Turner wrote, "The mystery of this pre-occupancy is far from being satisfactorily explained. It is an interesting, fruitful source of theories, enquiry and speculation."

And so it remains today.

# Tuscaroras in North Carolina

Much has been written about the history of the Tuscarora Indian Nation in western New York State, but their North Carolina sojourn is often overlooked. In 1708, the Tuscaroras inhabited North Carolina on the Neuse

River, but conflict with the colonists broke out in 1711. White immigrants moving into Indian Territory provoked the trouble.

The surveyor general of North Carolina, John Lawson, parceled out lots on Tuscarora land to give to white settlers. Lawson was accompanying Baron de Graffenried, showing him the lots, when the Tuscaroras captured them. They were taken to an Indian village and, before a general council, they were condemned to death. On the day of execution another general council was called and a reprieve was granted to Graffenried. He was kept as a prisoner, but Lawson was executed.

According to *Carroll's Historical Collections of South Carolina*, published in 1841, the Tuscaroras "took out redress of wrongs a little too severely upon Mr. Lawson, who, under color of being Surveyor General, had encroached too much upon their territory." The Indians then "way-laid him and cut his throat from ear to ear but at the same time released Baron de Graffenried, whom they had seized for company because it appeared plainly he had done no wrong."

A short time later, a band of Tuscarora and Coree Indians attacked scattered German settlers in the Roanoke area. Of this raid, the book said:

> *Becoming alarmed by this outrage they hoped to escape punishment by murdering on a given day all of the colonists south of Albermarle Sound. Dividing themselves into small parties, they commenced their horrid purpose on 22nd of September, 1711 on which memorable day 130 persons fell a sacrifice to their revenge.*

To put down this insurrection, aid was sought from South Carolina. A group from South Carolina came to assist the North Carolinians. The reinforcements included South Carolina militia with Cherokee, Creek and Catawba Indian allies. These Indians took arms against the Tuscaroras because they (the Tuscaroras) originated with the New York Iroquois, traditional enemies of the Southern tribes.

A peace was then negotiated, but it did not last long. The white encroachment continued, as did Tuscarora revenge raids. In December 1713 another South Carolina force invaded Tuscarora territory. The force contained some South Carolina militiamen, headed by Colonel James Moore, and a large number of Ashley Indians. They attacked a Tuscarora fort on the Neuse River and, according to Carroll's book, overran it. Inhabitants of the Tuscarora villages, of which there were about fifteen, were captured and sold into slavery.

Colonel Moore, according to the book, "in a few hours completely entered their works and 800 Tuscaroras became his prisoners. They were claimed by the Ashley Indians as a reward for their services and were taken to South Carolina where they were sold for slaves." After that, the legislature of North Carolina instituted a campaign whereby "men and money were raised and the woods were patrolled by the red allies who hunted for prisoners to be sold as slaves or took scalps for a reward."

The book said the Tuscaroras, "thus defeated and persecuted, driven from their lands and homes" by this aggression from "not only the colonial authorities but their own race," who "basely became the active allies of their enemies…migrated to New York." Upon reaching New York, the Tuscaroras were taken in by the Oneidas and later occupied the reservation land in the town of Lewiston, where they reside today.

Lockport historian Orsamus Turner said of the Tuscaroras, "Having been merged in the Iroquois confederacy, there is but little in their history since their arrival in this state of a distinctive character." He added, "We in fact mostly lose sight of them until the commencement of the Revolution." Turner noted that the Tuscaroras and Oneidas did not help the English in that great conflict; rather, they favored the colonists.

General John Sullivan, who led a campaign against the Iroquois when they were fighting for the English, in his written report had this to say of the friendly Indians:

> *Agreeable to my orders, I proceeded by the shortest route to the Lower Mohawk Castle, passing through the Tuscarora and Oneida Castles where every mark of hospitality and friendship was shown to the party. I had the pleasure to find that not the least damage nor insult was offered to any of the inhabitants.*

Turner also had some kind words for the Tuscaroras. He wrote:

> *The surviving pioneer settlers at Lewiston and its neighborhood bear witness to the uniform good conduct of the Tuscaroras and especially to the civility and hospitality they extended to the early drovers and other adventurers upon the trail that passed through their villages.*

# Midwinter Festival

Lockport residents had a unique way of celebrating the New Year in bygone days, but they were outshined by the Tuscarora Indians who honored a longstanding tradition with a daylong hunting contest and an eye-popping feast. Ladies used to hold open house in Lockport on New Year's Day while gentlemen toured the city, going from house to house to sample the food and socialize. It was a good way for singles to meet and, perhaps, start a lasting romance. The Tuscaroras used the New Year as an occasion to uphold an old Iroquois religious tradition of putting on a midwinter feast. One such event in the late 1930s was aptly described by Tuscarora Wolf Clan Chief Ted C. Williams in his book *The Reservation*.

I had the occasion to interview Williams and write about his book on March 21, 1976, when I was in the Niagara Falls Bureau of the now defunct *Buffalo Courier-Express*. Syracuse University Press published Williams's book that year.

Williams, who was fluent in the Tuscarora language, said the big feast on New Year's Day was preceded by a daylong hunting contest between old men and the youth of the reservation. All the game was cooked for the feast, along with a ton of other food that had been prepared by Indian families, and was taken to the feast in wagons. Williams said he was captain of the youth team, and an old man he named "Bee-Land" headed the old men's team. The winner was determined not only by which team caught the most game (crows and mice were not counted), but also by who excelled in a debate held after the hunt.

Williams, who hunted with bow and arrow as well as shotguns, told of a unique Tuscarora way of catching rabbits. First, he instructed, look for a brush pile with a hole in the snow leading underneath it. Pin up the sleeve of a jacket and lay the jacket over the hole. Stomp on the woodpile so the rabbit runs into the jacket and into the sleeve with the end pinned and, he said, "Bingo! Rabbit pie."

About 8:00 p.m., all headed to the Reservation Council House where "a couple hundred Indians were in sight" and huge kettles of water for cooking were being boiled over open fires. As he approached the scene, Williams wrote, he shouted, "Hey, what's going on here?"

A voice replied, "We ain't celebratin' Columbus Day!"

The teams gathered around a long table and took turns pulling game out of bags until more than a hundred animals were on the table. The game included rabbits, squirrels, raccoons and pheasants, and even one deer had been killed. This would all go into the pots for potpies.

The feast came in several servings and seconds were encouraged. Williams said, "Eat more right away because others are jammed at the door waiting for the next serving." There were also sporting events outside for those who had finished eating.

Finally came the big debate between a representative from each team. The speakers had three cracks at the appreciative audience. The debate over who won the contest mostly involved insults directed at the opposing team.

The speaker for the youngsters said his team had clearly won and should pity the old men. He said, "During the summer we should take them by the hand and lead them to where the game lives and say, 'This is a hunting ground.'"

When the representative of the old men had his turn, he said he once pulled a fencepost out and later saw his adversary over the hole. Asked what he was doing, the youngster replied, "I found this hole and I'm gonna get that fox too!"

There were also Indian songs and dances by both men and women. A couple of dance teams came from other reservations.

Williams concluded, "Everyone in the Council House could feel that the Midwinter Festival was almost over with for one whole year. The hunt and debate were all part of the celebration and whoever brought in the most pieces of game, young or old, didn't really matter."

# Handsome Lake

The Seneca prophet Handsome Lake (1735–1815), founder of an Indian religious movement that gained widespread acceptance, turned a dissipated and wasteful life into a model of morality. He was born in the Seneca village of Conawaga on the Genesee River opposite present-day Avon. And he was a half brother of the celebrated Seneca Chief Cornplanter.

Anthropologist Arthur C. Parker, a great-grandson of Seneca Chief Ely S. Parker, who was secretary to General Ulysses S. Grant, studied extensively the works of Handsome Lake because, he wrote, "The success of Handsome Lake's teaching did much to crystallize the Iroquois as a distinct social group."

Little is known of Handsome Lake's life, Parker said, but he is recognized mostly through his teachings as outlined in his code. "It is known from tradition and from his own story," Parker wrote, "that he was a dissolute person and a miserable victim of the drink habit."

It is little wonder, then, that first among Handsome Lake's moral teachings was complete abstinence from the white man's firewater. He had some "wasting disease," aggravated by years of drinking, and "for four years he lay a helpless invalid." Later, his married daughter nursed him.

It was at this time that he had a near-death experience and had celestial visions. In the foreword of his revelation he tells how he was near death and was visited by four beings that revealed to him the will of the Creator.

Chief Cornplanter also wrote of his half brother, whom he called Ganiodaiio. He said that Handsome Lake fell dying as his daughter caught him at the cabin door. But, as mourners came, some noticed "warm blood [was] pulsing in his veins. Now his breath comes and now he opens his eyes."

Handsome Lake then told the startled mourners, "Never have I seen such wondrous visions." He told of the four messengers from the Creator and the many things they told him to do.

The messengers said, "Do not allow anyone to say that you have had great fortune in being able to rise again. The favor of the four beings is not alone for you and the Creator is willing to help all mankind."

Handsome Lake began traveling among the Iroquois villages preaching his new code, which seemed to borrow much from the teachings of Christianity. Parker wrote, "In two years' time his efforts were conducive of so much reform that they attracted the attention of President Jefferson who caused Secretary of War Dearborn to write a letter commending the teachings of Handsome Lake."

Dearborn's letter stated in part:

> *Brothers, if all the red people follow the advice of your friend and teacher Handsome Lake and in future will be sober, honest, industrious and good, there can be no doubt but the Great Spirit will take care of you and make you happy.*

Like most prophets, Handsome Lake met much resistance at first. One of his chief protagonists was Seneca Chief Red Jacket who "denounced him as an imposter." In retaliation, Handsome Lake said the messengers revealed to him that "Red Jacket was a schemer and a seller of land and an unhappy wretch doomed to carry burdens of soil through eternity as a punishment for perfidy."

Chief Cornplanter wrote about his half brother, "He made mistakes, many mistakes, so it is reported, but he was only a man and men are liable to commit errors." He added that Handsome Lake did not claim to be divine or infallible "nor even truly virtuous…We do not worship him, we worship one great Creator. We honor and revere our prophet and leader, we revere the four messengers who watch over, but the Creator alone do we worship."

# Big Tree Treaty

Robert Morris, probably the richest man in America when he financed the Revolutionary War, was an old man in extremely dire straits when he squared off against the Seneca Indians negotiating the infamous Big Tree Treaty.

Morris, who owned all of western New York at one time, was a signer of the Declaration of Independence, a confidante of George Washington and a very rich man. He gained much of his riches operating privateer boats during the Revolutionary War. Privateers attacked and boarded English merchant ships and confiscated all their cargo.

After the war, he turned to land speculation with an overriding passion and it became his downfall. Historian Henry W. Clune, in his book *The Genesee*, said Morris was making his last stand for solvency when the treaty was negotiated in 1797. Clune wrote, "He was 67 at the time of Big Tree; he had five more years to live, and three of these were to be passed in the Prune Street jail for debtors in Philadelphia."

Due to ill health, Robert Morris did not attend the negotiations, but instead sent his son Tom, who approached the session with great expectations. The Senecas, likewise, anticipated the council session, but for different reasons. Most were now reluctant to give up any more of their land to the white man, but they converged on the hamlet of Big Tree expecting that "big kettles would be hung" and there would be "a feast of fat things" and much free rum.

Big Tree, now Geneseo, was located on the Genesee River just north of the present-day Letchworth State Park. The Genesee Valley was the traditional home of the Seneca Nation.

The land transactions of that period were quite complicated. While New York State eventually got sovereignty over state land, Massachusetts claimed title to it. Morris bought all of western New York from Massachusetts, but the sale was contingent upon gaining title from the Senecas, the true owners.

Morris had struck the deal with Massachusetts, but he still needed Indian approval. In the meantime, he sold much of the land to Theophile Cazenove, an agent for the Holland Land Company, but could not get his money until he had cleared the title from the Senecas. He hoped to make enough from the deal to satisfy his creditors.

Hundreds of Indians, many famous Iroquois sachems, or chiefs, attended the meeting and watched Tom Morris start the council fire as negotiations began. Robert Morris had written to his son instructing him to ply the Indians with food and gifts, but to withhold the whiskey until a treaty was signed. Tom Morris offered $75,000 for about four million acres of land. The Senecas, who had been bested in questionable negotiations by Oliver Phelps and Nathaniel Gorham when they sold most of their land east of the Genesee, were resolved to keep all of their land west of the river.

The negotiations were stalemated. A recess was called, and the next day Morris offered $100,000, but the great Seneca orator Red Jacket said the Indians had already lost much of their traditional land and no amount of money could make them part with any more. The Seneca Chief Cornplanter asked Morris to check his Bible to see if the white man's Great Spirit directed them to intrude on Indian property.

Morris provided feasts of ox roasts and passed out gifts of knives and blankets. But, on his father's advice, he withheld the whiskey in the hope that the Senecas would look forward to the alcoholic party and give in to his entreaties.

Red Jacket, who was noted for his fondness for hard drink, remained steadfast and the rest of the Senecas listened to his silver-tongued oration against any land giveaway.

Robert Morris, unable to attend the enclave because of sickness, wrote a letter to the Senecas that his son delivered. He wrote:

> *My brothers of the Seneca Nation, it was my wish and my intentions to have come into your country and to have met with you at this treaty, but the Great Spirit ordained otherwise.*
>
> *Brothers, it is now six years since I have been invested with the exclusive right to acquire your lands, during the whole of which time, you have quietly possessed them without being importuned to sell them, but I now think that it is time for them to be productive to you.*

Tom Morris worked hard to save his father's crumbling financial empire. One of his ploys was to try to convince the Senecas of the benefits of bank interest. Such a concept was foreign to the Native Americans. Morris said if he "planted" the $100,000 he was offering for the four million acres, they would reap $6,000 a year in interest. But the Seneca chiefs had no interest in "growing" money. They wanted to keep their land.

Morris then tried to impress them with what a large amount $100,000 was. He said if it were in silver, it would take thirty horses to pull it in a wagon from Philadelphia to the Genesee country.

The Senecas, led by the picturesque oratory of Red Jacket, remained adamant. At that point, Red Jacket extinguished the council fire and proclaimed negotiations to be over.

Tom Morris was resolute. During an adjournment, he turned to the Seneca women, who wielded much power in the Iroquois system. The clan mothers chose the chiefs. He showered them with gifts and said the money would improve their lives.

After a few days of feasting and frolicking, some sachems urged Morris to reopen the negotiations. They said that since he had first lighted the council fire, Red Jacket had had no authority to extinguish it. Only the person who started the fire could put it out.

With the women on his side and Red Jacket sleeping off some drink under a tree, Morris wheedled agreement from the sachems. But there remained the question of reservation land for the Indians.

At that point, the legendary white Indian woman Mary Jemison addressed the council. Captured by the Indians as a youngster, she had decided to remain a Seneca. She asked that the treaty provide land for her along the Genesee. Morris finally acceded to her pleas and she received nearly eighteen thousand acres at Gardeau Flats, now the site of Letchworth State Park.

The deed of conveyance contained both tribal names and English names of the chiefs next to which they were to affix their Xs. Red Jacket even acquiesced and became a signatory along with Handsome Lake, Hot Bread, Cornplanter, Tall Chief, Farmer's Brother and Little Billy, to name a few of the fifty-two sachems who signed the deed.

When the whiskey was gone, the Senecas left Big Tree and Robert Morris had his profit, but still not enough to restore his fiscal solvency. The rapidly encroaching white settlers eventually pushed the Senecas onto the reservations.

The treaty promised them reservation land "forever, so long as trees grow and rivers run." But that promise was hollow and the land grab has continued even into modern times.

# PART II

# Wars

# Devil's Hole Massacre

The fatal attack by some Seneca Indians took place on September 14, 1763, when a wagon train traveling from Fort Schlosser to the Lewiston Landing on the upper Niagara River was waylaid at Devil's Hole along the gorge. All but three of the twenty-five escorts of the wagon train were slain.

It was a horrific and gory scene. Horses bucked in panic as wagons lurched out of control. Confusion and terror were the order of the hour. The few who surrendered were slain on the spot; fierce Seneca warriors were taking no prisoners. The precipice of Devil's Hole became a slaughter scene.

The Indian contingent congregated before dawn to take up positions in the woods, behind trees and thickets, at the narrow bridge over the creek near the place called Devil's Hole. Just over the gorge there was a cave that howled like demons when the wind blew. The Indians from years and years before had named it the Devil's Hole because of the frequent bad luck and many native deaths associated with the place. The Devil's Hole would be a fitting site to wreak carnage on the English. And the narrow bridge, plus the thick nearby cover, would make it an excellent ambush site.

Early on the morning of September 14, Portage Master John Stedman, with a lieutenant and about twenty-five soldiers, including one young Canadian drummer boy, made ready to return the nearly empty wagons from Fort Schlosser to Fort Niagara. Lumbering oxen drew most of the wagons, but draft horses pulled a few. Stedman led the contingent on his favorite stallion. Because the trip up with the supplies had brought no attack, Stedman was sure the return trip would be a cakewalk.

Stedman's horse clapped over the wooden bridge at the Devil's Hole slightly before noon. When he was over the bridge and up the trail a short distance, he stopped his horse and turned in the saddle to check the progress of the wagon train behind him. Some of the drivers had dismounted from their wagons to lead the oxen. Others ambled lazily along. Stedman whistled to them and waved them on to hurry the procession along. He was anxious to get to the fort.

At the first piercing war cry of the raiding party, Stedman froze. The entire wagon train froze in fear. The Indian war cries were accompanied by the blasts of muskets. Men fell; blood splattered. It took Stedman only a few seconds to realize they were under attack. With fear squeezing his heart and enveloping his stomach, he whirled in his saddle, dug his heels into the side of the stallion and took off thundering down the portage trail with bullets and arrows whizzing past his ears. Instead of riding to the military encampment at Lewiston Landing ahead, he whirled to the east and rode through the forest all the way to Gill Creek and then to the Niagara River and back to the safety of Fort Schlosser.

He was the only one able to escape, but the young drummer boy, whose drum strap snagged on a tree limb as he was tossed into the gorge, also survived and managed to climb back to the top long after the massacre was over. There were some unconfirmed reports that a third soldier escaped by hiding in a thicket.

The battle was prompted by Pontiac's War, the effort of Chief Pontiac to drive the white man into the sea and out of Native American lives forever.

Several historians note that some Senecas, who had earned money carrying goods over the portage, were upset at being fired when Portage Master Stedman improved the trail and instituted the use of wagons to haul the goods. Some say it was the first instance of labor unrest in the nation.

But Pontiac's successes (and excesses) in the siege of Fort Detroit no doubt played a big part in leading up to the portage massacre. The portage was the only lifeline transporting goods to the upper Great Lakes, and cutting off that lifeline would have been a great help to Pontiac's siege of Fort Detroit.

The area's top administrator, Lord Jeffrey Amherst, had also infuriated the Senecas. Amherst, who despised Indians, decided against appeasing Indians with gifts and instituted harsh treatment instead.

When Pontiac tried to rally the Iroquois to his cause, Sir William Johnson went to great lengths to keep the western New York Indians on the side of the British. Mohawk War Chief Joseph Brant and his sister Molly (Johnson's live-in companion who bore him several children) aided in persuading the majority of Iroquois Nations to remain loyal to the British.

The soldiers encamped at Lewiston heard the musket fire and piercing war cries of the Indians and the terrified screams of the victims. Two officers, Lieutenant William Frazier and Lieutenant George Campbell, led a contingent of about eighty soldiers of the Eightieth Regiment of Light Armed Foot. They grabbed up muskets and raced up the portage trail to rescue their fellow soldiers.

They, too, were ambushed and most were slain.

Old Stone Chimney as it exists today in Porter Park, Niagara Falls. It was built in 1740 at Fort Schlosser in the upper Niagara River area.

A report from Captain George Etherington read:

> *Major Wilkins with all the 60th Regiment that were here set out to support Mr. Campbell but on our arrival at the little landing we were informed by two soldiers that the two companies were entirely cut down and the Indians were very numerous, some said five hundred and some said four. Major Wilkins stayed at the little landing till the arrival of reinforcement from the 46th should arrive. But before they came it was night and it was then thought too late to proceed. Accordingly, we all came back to the fort that night and set off next morning very early. When we came up to the graves we found Lieutenant Campbell and sixteen men on the road, all stripped, disemboweled and scalped and thirty two more*

Ottawa Chief Pontiac
started Pontiac's War to
drive the white man into
the sea.

Sir William Johnson,
Indian agent for the
British in New York State
during the time of the
Devil's Hole massacre.

*in the same situation which the enemy had thrown down the rocks, which with what men we found dead afterwards we can make out seventy six men killed and eight or nine wounded. By everything we can learn, this was done by the Senecas.*

# Peter B. Porter

Peter B. Porter, a member of the first influential Niagara Falls business family, was a politician turned soldier who became a legitimately brave hero of the War of 1812.

Governor Daniel D. Tompkins made Porter a brigadier general in the New York State militia after the war broke out in June of 1812. In those days, officers in state militias were named because of political connections. Even officers in the regular army were often rewarded for political connections rather than military ability. But Porter rose to the military occasion.

General Porter, a resident of Black Rock near Buffalo at that time, was a lawyer and a partner with his brother, Augustus Porter, in operating the portage and conducting extensive real estate dealings in all of downtown Niagara Falls. He was elected to Congress and was a noted War Hawk in deliberations leading to a declaration of war. He resigned from Congress to enter combat.

Author Richard V. Barbuto, a retired lieutenant colonel in the army with a doctorate in history, wrote extensively of Porter in his chronicle of the war, *Niagara 1814*. Although he had no formal military training, Porter's instincts were keen. Barbuto noted that Porter, from the beginning, advocated a quick strike against Quebec by volunteers, who, unlike state militia, could not refuse to fight outside of the United States.

Porter recognized the strategic importance of Quebec and the Saint Lawrence River to "Upper Canada," as the area just across the Niagara River was called. However, President James Madison and Secretary of War John Armstrong decided to initiate fighting in the Detroit area, which turned into a humiliating American defeat.

The first invasion of Canada from this area in 1812 also turned into a disaster. The Americans appeared victorious at the battle of Queenston Heights, during which Canadian Major General Sir Isaac Brock was killed.

General Peter B. Porter,
the younger brother of
Augustus, was a hero in the
War of 1812.

Augustus Porter, a pioneer
settler of Niagara Falls and
a partner in the operation
of the portage. He owned
most of the land around
the falls.

A War of 1812 reenactment at Old Fort Niagara.

But British reinforcements and Mohawk Indians turned the battle into a British victory. Thousands of New York State militiamen at Lewiston Landing, on seeing the slaughter across the river, refused to leave the country to aid their comrades trapped in Canada. The militia, under Porter, was to redeem itself later in the war. The British later avenged the Canadian invasion by attacking Fort Niagara, taking control of it and laying waste to most of the American settlements all the way to Buffalo.

Later that year, Regular Army General Alexander Smyth, in charge of Niagara Frontier forces, planned an invasion of Canada from Black Rock. General Porter and his militia were among twenty-six hundred troops already in boats, with another two thousand waiting onshore to get in boats, when Smyth called off the attack ostensibly because of bad weather.

Smyth's indecision caused several other cancellations of the invasion. Barbuto wrote, "Porter publicly ascribed the debacle to the cowardice of General Smyth. Porter withdrew this charge only after he and Smyth exchanged shots in a duel seven days later."

On July 11, 1813, the British crossed the river and raided Black Rock. They burned a small schooner at the naval yard there. Barbuto wrote, "Porter organized a force of regulars, militiamen and Senecas to drive off the raiders. The Senecas were about to scalp the British dead but were prevented from doing so by Porter." Porter's friendships with Seneca Chiefs Red Jacket, Cornplanter and Farmer's Brother aided him in convincing the warriors to join the American cause.

Porter's bravest exploits, and the bloodiest fighting, took place in 1814 at the battles of Chippewa, Lundy's Lane and Fort Erie.

At the battle of Chippewa on July 5, 1814, the forces were under command of Major General Jacob Brown, who had been in the militia but was elevated to regular army status. General Winfield Scott, who went on in later years to head the entire U.S. Army, aided him.

Barbuto wrote about that battle:

> *Porter did well, considering that his Iroquois and militiamen had not trained together. Given the mission to clear the enemy from the deep and dense woods, Porter chose an appropriate formation and moved with a sense of urgency. He probably knew that he would lose control once heavy contact was made, but that is the nature of forest warfare.*

In the dense woods, they eventually encountered combat-hardened British regulars and their Indian allies, fierce Mohawk warriors. Porter, in a letter to Governor Tompkins about the battle, wrote, "I rallied and led a scattered line [formed to scour the woods and not to fight a regular force] exhausted by troops perfectly fresh [the British] by which I lost several valuable officers." Porter was upset because regular army officers and troops always got to the front of battles first and, of course, had the best crack at glory.

Barbuto wrote that, at the battle of Chippewa, "Porter was irritated that Brown [Major General Jacob Brown, commanding] had the Third Brigade [led by Porter] bringing up the rear; however, he hid it well." Before that battle, in March of 1814, New York Governor Tompkins ordered the raising of about twenty-seven hundred volunteers for six months' service. He named Porter to head this group, "a fortunate choice," Barbuto wrote, "though unschooled in the technical aspects of military operations, Porter was well respected, intelligent, and like Brown and Scott, whom he would eventually join, aggressive and brave."

In a later letter to Tompkins, Porter complained that it seemed an officer had to be in the regular army in order to get into the thick of battles or to get any credit. But Porter's chance soon came in the seesaw battle of Lundy's Lane in Canada, not far from Chippewa. Barbuto called that battle the bloodiest of the war and as ferocious as any of the Civil War.

The Americans, led by Brigadier General Winfield Scott, swarmed to a ridge on Lundy's Lane that was fortified with cannon. The first phase was the fight of the First Brigade, under Scott, to take the ridge before the arrival of reinforcements. The second phase was the arrival of General Ripley's and General Porter's brigades. The last phase was the unsuccessful, but incessant, British counterattacks to regain the crest of the ridge.

After the initial clash, Porter arrived with his brigade, which was diminished from fighting at Chippewa. He took about three hundred men and marched them to the left of the American line, south of Lundy's Lane, to protect the flank.

The fighting was fierce. The British, driven off their ridge, attacked repeatedly to regain their cannons. Much of the fighting was at close range, both with muskets and bayonets. A musket ball could do as much damage to a body as a modern hollow point slug. Barbuto wrote:

> *The thirsty, exhausted Americans prepared as best they could in the forty-five minutes between the second and third counterattacks. The American line was bent back into a horseshoe. Too many officers were wounded or dead.*

The commander, General Brown, was also wounded and removed to Chippewa. At nightfall, the British halted their attack. The Americans then withdrew to Chippewa. Brown ordered Brigadier General Ripley to return to the Lundy's Lane ridge and take control of the British cannons, but, for some reason, Ripley refused the order.

Brown was evacuated to a hospital in Williamsville. Ripley not only refused the order, but he also decided to give up his strong defensive position behind the Chippewa River. He wanted to return to Black Rock, but Porter and other officers "vehemently protested," Barbuto wrote, and the troops remained at Fort Erie.

That fall, the British, bolstered by reinforcements, moved to retake Fort Erie and set up a siege. Porter played a major role in breaking that siege. On September 17, 1814, Barbuto wrote, "Porter started forming his men southwest of Snake Hill in midmorning and gave a stirring speech in which he presented his plan of attack." They left the fort and overran, in a driving rain, British Battery Three. They disabled the cannons and moved toward Battery Two.

According to Barbuto:

> *By all reports the New Yorkers fought like regulars. Many of the rain soaked muskets would not fire and the men resorted to cold steel or using their weapons as clubs. Porter received a sword cut to his hand and was momentarily captured, but a small party led by a sergeant rescued him.*

Although the Americans won that battle, they later voluntarily left Fort Erie and returned to Black Rock. The Treaty of Ghent ended the war, basically in a tie.

After the war, acting Secretary of War James Monroe, in downsizing the army, wanted to keep the best officers and, of course, he kept Jacob Brown and Winfield Scott in high positions. Barbuto noted that Monroe also said "that President Madison would give Porter a commission as a Major General in the regular army—certainly a mark of confidence in Porter."

However, Porter declined and returned to his business interests in Niagara Falls.

# Cowardly Militia

When speaking of the United States military it is considered patriotic to use words such as noble, selfless and brave, but, on rare occasion, the citizen army has exhibited cowardice en masse. A couple of instances of this disagreeable subject came right here on the Niagara frontier during the War of 1812 when the United States took on the powerhouse Great Britain for the second time in thirty-six years.

The first instance occurred during the battle for Queenston on October 13, 1812, when U.S. troops, mostly untrained state militia, invaded Canada. The attack went well at first for the U.S. troops, who took Queenston Heights and even killed Major General Sir Isaac Brock, the governor of Canada. However, a vicious attack by the British and Indians to retake the heights proved successful. American militia reinforcements, still on the shoreline at Lewiston, refused to take boats across the Niagara River to help their routed comrades in Canada.

The state militia, afraid of the fierce British and Indian fighters, refused the order to attack Canada on the grounds that the state militia was not required to fight outside of the state. In his report, the Fort Niagara commander who ordered the invasion, Major General Stephen Van Ranselaer, said the United States could have won the battle if the reinforcements had crossed the river and joined the attack as ordered.

The other incidents of U.S. militia cowardice came at the end of the next year, on December 29, 1813, when the British attacked the villages of Black Rock and Buffalo. This incident was well covered by Lockport newspaper editor and historian Orsamus Turner in his *Pioneer History of the Holland Purchase* published in 1849.

The invaders captured an artillery position in Black Rock with little resistance and then headed toward Buffalo. United States General Amos Hall, in his report to Governor Daniel D. Tompkins, wrote that most of the militia supporting the few regular army troops fled. The United States, according to some accounts, had nearly three thousand men while the British attacked with a thousand troops under Major General Phineas Riall.

In his later report, Hall wrote that the enemy "opened a heavy fire upon us of shells, hot shot and ball. The whole force now opposed to the enemy was, at most not over 600 men, the remainder having fled in spite of the exertions of their officers." He said the remaining regulars fought bravely, but were overwhelmed by sheer numbers. He wrote, "Deserted by my principal force, I fell back that night to Eleven Mile Creek and was forced to leave the flourishing villages of Black Rock and Buffalo to the enemy."

Turner, himself a youth during this destruction, witnessed the flight of both militia and citizens that took place. He wrote, "Of the stirring and diversified scenes of flight and refuge presented upon the south route, via Willink [Aurora] and the old Big Tree Road on the 30th of December, the author is enabled to give some account from personal observation and recollection." In a disgraceful scene, Turner wrote that "squads of armed soldiers in many instances preceded even women and children in the hasty retreat." He added, "It was odd enough and disgraceful enough but it was nevertheless a fact that retreating soldiers and even some officers as they arrived in the back settlements added to the panic and dismay."

After the debacle, President Madison sent General Lewis Cass to investigate and report what had happened. In his written report to the secretary of war, General Cass said, "The force of the enemy has been greatly magnified. From the most careful examination I am satisfied that not more than 650 of regulars, militia and Indians landed at Black Rock. To oppose these we had 2,500 to 3,000 militia." About the U.S. militia, he wrote, "All except a very few of them behaved in the most cowardly manner. They fled without discharging a musket."

Turner said there was one continuous line of refugees fleeing along the road, including "retreating soldiers, men, women and children from Buffalo, families from the settlements in all the southern portion of what is now Erie County and the Indians en masse from the Buffalo Reservation." He added, "Bread, meats and drinks soon vanished from the log taverns on the routes and the stationary and fleeing settlers divided their scant stores with the almost famished that came from the frontiers."

However, Turner said, the militia was somewhat vindicated that summer when it broke the British siege of Fort Erie under an attack led by General Porter. Fighting side by side with his men, Porter was slightly wounded and captured but later freed by his troops during the sortie. The U.S. militia also distinguished itself in the battles of Chippewa and Lundy's Lane in Canada. Turner wrote, "The gallant conduct of the volunteers…at the sortie of Fort Erie goes far to redeem the character of our local militia, so tarnished and forfeited by cowardice and flight."

# Patriots' War

The Patriots' War in the nineteenth century was mainly a Canadian issue, but the United States, especially Niagara County, was heavily involved in the brief and abortive conflict. Niagara County sites, as well as Canadian Navy Island, played prominent roles in the conflict. The only participant in the rebellion to be hanged was a U.S. citizen, and a U.S. ship, the *Caroline*, was burned and sent over the falls.

The Navy Island and *Caroline* involvements in the Patriots' War have been well documented on this side of the river, but many interesting Canadian connections just across the border are not as well known. Canadian historian Colin K. Duquemin reveals many more interesting incidents about the Patriots' War in his book *Niagara Rebels*.

Perhaps the prime instigator in the rebellion was William Lyon Mackenzie, a Scotch immigrant who started a newspaper in Queenston just across the river.

His editorial stance was mild at first, but it soon evolved into strong criticism of government practices that earned him the nickname "the Firebrand."

Mackenzie moved to York (now Toronto) in the fall of 1824 and continued citing grievances until he eventually led a rebellion in 1837. Failing there, he went to Buffalo to recruit an army to take Canada back from British control. He issued a proclamation promising recruits three hundred acres "of the most valuable land in Canada" and "$100 in silver payable on or before the 1st of May next." A sizeable army was raised and they took over Navy Island in the upper Niagara River near Grand Island, then occupied by only one family.

The late Niagara County historian Clarence O. Lewis wrote that Lockport resident Major Benajah Mallory, a veteran of the Revolutionary War and the War of 1812, was asked to take over the army. However, he refused because the action was not approved by the U.S. government, which did not relish yet another war with Britain.

The *Caroline*, which was used to ferry arms and ammunition from Schlosser Landing, a few miles above the falls, to Navy Island, was attacked while docked at Schlosser the night of December 29, 1837. Commander Andrew Drew of the Canadian army led seven boats with forty-five men on the commando raid.

The *Caroline*'s ten-man crew, and about thirty-two others who could not find lodging at Schlosser, were sleeping on the boat that night when it was captured. All fled to shore. But one American, Captain Amos Durfee, was shot and killed in the mêlée. The *Caroline* was set on fire and sent over the falls.

This caused uproar in the United States and nearly precipitated an all-out war. A Niagara County grand jury indicted Canadian Alexander McLeod for killing Durfee. McLeod was later caught in Lewiston, tried in Utica and freed on a technicality.

Mackenzie, who could not get along with Patriot military leader Rennselaer Van Rennselaer, left the area to try to rouse support in other areas of the state. Meanwhile, Navy Island was abandoned and the rebellion lost steam for a while.

It picked up again in mid-March 1838 when a group called the Canadian Refugee Relief Association was formed in Lockport and invasion plans began anew. A very brief skirmish took place in the Short Hills area of Canada, located at the end of Lundy's Lane not far from the falls.

The association included "General" Donald McLeod, a former sergeant in the British army, and Colonel James Morreau, a tanner from Girard, Pennsylvania. Others who figured prominently in the invasion were Lieutenants Benjamin Wait and Samuel Chandler, who, other than Morreau,

William Lyon Mackenzie was the driving force behind the Patriots' War to free Canada from British control.

The U.S. ship *Caroline* was attacked and burned by the British and sent over the falls during the Patriots' War in 1837.

suffered most from the abortive rebellion. And there was the tale of Canadian Edward Seymour, who claimed he was "abducted" in Manchester (now Niagara Falls) and forced by Patriot forces to participate in the invasion.

History does not relate whether Seymour was a willing participant in the Patriots' War of rebellion to free Canada from Britain, or whether he was a cowardly liar intent on saving his own skin. The story, as related by Seymour and recorded in official Canadian trial documents, leaves the final decision up to the reader.

After the initial instigator, William Lyon Mackenzie, left the movement in this area, others continued the battle to free Canada. Seymour became a key player. At later trials, he told the court that he left Canada about May 1, 1868, to visit an uncle in Palmyra, New York. On his way back to Canada, he stopped in Manchester (now Niagara Falls) and was accosted on the road by four men with pistols and swords on about June 18.

Earlier, on June 7, Morreau, who listed himself as commander in chief, issued a proclamation saying, "Canadians—We have at last been successful in planting the standards of liberty in one part of our oppressed country—Fort George and Fort Missisauga are now in our possession." This was a complete fabrication.

Seymour, continuing with his tale, said these men, members of the Patriot's army, "arrested" him and took him to a house at the mouth of Cayuga Creek, in the LaSalle section of Niagara Falls, a rallying point for the Patriots' army to take boats to Navy Island and Canada. He said if he had not taken an oath to the Patriots' cause, he would have been put to death.

Of course he joined the Patriot band.

Then, he said, two guards rowed him to Buckhorn Island off Grand Island and ordered him to gather up arms and ammunition cached there, load them in a boat and take the stores to Navy Island. The next night, the munitions, along with an invasion force, crossed the river to an area near Chippewa. The invaders then moved inland a short distance, Seymour said, and met a Patriot commander, "who was a stout man, rather tall with dark curly hair and dark complexioned by name of Morreau." Seymour said he was ordered to take up a musket and join the Patriots' army in night combat attack.

Morreau had been promised three hundred reinforcements by General McLeod on Navy Island, but, at the moment, Morreau had only forty men. Meanwhile, Canadian forces, ever vigilant since the rebellion began, moved up troops to the Niagara frontier.

The Patriot troops, edgy from hiding within Canada, were spoiling for an attack against the village of Saint Johns in the Short Hills area, but Colonel

Benjamin Wait was a major
participant in the Patriots' War.

Morreau was wary. He and Samuel Chandler, disappointed because no
reinforcements appeared, wanted to move back to the American side. But a
majority of the troops did not want to leave Canada without making a strike.
Morreau stepped down as commander but agreed to go along as a private, as
did Chandler. Jacob Beamer assumed command and an attack commenced
on the evening of June 20.

On the way, they plundered the homes of Abraham Overholt and his son
Martin. They arrived at Saint Johns in the early morning hours of Friday,
June 21, and attacked Osterhout's Tavern, which served as an outpost for ten
Canadian dragoons. Major Benjamin Wait was among the first attackers who
broke down the door. Musket balls smashed into the building. Some fired up
from the first floor to the Canadian troops billeted on the second floor.

About 3:00 a.m., Sergeant Bailey of the Canadian dragoons realized they
were short on powder and balls and, hearing the Patriots threaten to torch
the building, decided to surrender. The raiders, after savoring their victory,

decided it would be best to make it to the American shore. The battle resulted in more than fifty rounds fired into the tavern. Three dragoons were wounded and one killed. Two Patriots were also wounded.

Word of the attack had reached Saint Catharines and the Lincoln Calvary was sent out, followed by infantry units. They hunted down the rebels for three days before capturing the insurgents, and then followed the interesting trials on charges of treason for the Canadians, and on the waging of an illegal war for the Americans in the Patriots' army. The trials were held in the courthouse at Niagara (now Niagara-on-the-lake, Canada), across the mouth of the Niagara River from Youngstown, New York. American James Morreau's trial for illegally invading Canada with the Patriots' army began on Saturday, July 21, 1838.

Solicitor General William Henry Draper prosecuted the cases. Morreau was provided a defense counsel, James Boulton, and the judge was Justice Jonas Jones. The courtroom was packed as the list of witnesses began taking the stand.

The indictment charged Morreau with violating the recently passed law entitled an "Act to protect the inhabitants of this Province against lawless aggressions from subjects of foreign countries at peace with Her Majesty." James Edy, the soldier who had captured Morreau on June 26 at an inn near the Grand River, said Morreau at first gave his name as Morrison and said he was traveling from Queenston to Chatham. Edy, being suspicious, had arrested him and taken him to Colonel Townshend. According to official notes of the judge, Morreau was recognized on the way, at which point he gave his true name to the colonel and said he was a native of Pennsylvania.

The next witness, Edward Seymour, told his tale of being abducted in Manchester and taken to Morreau at a house at the mouth of Cayuga Creek. He identified Morreau as well as other participants in the raid at Saint Johns. Seymour may have turned state's evidence to protect himself, but, under cross-examination, he insisted that he had acted through compulsion. According to the judge's notes, Seymour testified that "he was always watched. He would have made his escape if he could. Orders were given that if anyone attempted to escape he was to be shot." But when Seymour was first apprehended after the raid, "he gave a false account of himself," as Seymour later said, "to avoid trouble."

Robert Bailey, a sergeant in the Queen's Lancers who commanded the small detachment at Saint Johns, testified that he saw Morreau in the street after the detachment surrendered. He testified that Morreau "seemed to have command of the party and was called Colonel. He was armed with a belt having a brace of pistols and a rifle with a white ribbon in his hat and an eagle feather."

After a parade of fourteen witnesses, the jury retired, but it returned in about two minutes with a guilty verdict. Justice Jonas Jones sentenced Morreau to be hanged on Monday, July 30, outside the courthouse, which also served as the jail. Newspaper accounts noted, "Morreau displayed much firmness only slightly agitated when he received his sentence."

Justice Jones later wrote, "The evidence upon which he was convicted was most clear and satisfactory—so much so that his counsel gave up the defense upon the facts admitting that the jury could do no otherwise than convict."

Linus Miller, a compatriot who shared the cell with Morreau, said the condemned man's last words were, "I die a martyr to a righteous cause and I die happy. Death has no sting, for I shall soon wear a crown of glory."

The *Niagara Chronicle*, a Canadian paper, in writing about the hanging said Morreau moved his lips in silent prayer as the trap was sprung and he "paid his debt to nature and mankind without a struggle."

The newspaper was stingingly critical of a Lewiston newspaper for instigating Morreau to join the rebellion. The *Chronicle* reporter wrote, "Where shall we find terms indignant enough to express our feelings toward the *Lewiston Telegraph*, the malignant, hell-born lines of that paper having contributed to induce Morreau to unite himself with the cause."

Another Canadian paper, the *Niagara Reporter*, said, "The guilt of Morreau's death is most emphatically on the head of the conductor of the *Lewiston Telegraph* because by the unparalleled mendacity of that print he was seduced into crime."

The *Chronicle* also wrote about the large crowd that witnessed the hanging and commented on the large number of women there. "We allude to the number of respectably dressed females who seemed collected there for the purpose of beholding some pleasurable sight." The paper noted, "In the Old Country no females attend such spectacles except those of totally depraved and wanton habits."

Both Samuel Chandler and Benjamin Wait, being Canadians and British subjects, were indicted for high treason and their trials followed the pattern of James Morreau's trial. The trials were held in the courthouse at Niagara, with the same judge, prosecutor and defense counsel.

Nine witnesses appeared against Chandler, and this time the defense called five witnesses. The jury deliberated "a very considerable time" before returning a guilty verdict with a recommendation for mercy. Benjamin Wait's trial followed on August 3, but this time the defense counsel was Alexander

Stewart. There were eight witnesses for the prosecution and none called for the defense. The jury returned a guilty verdict with a recommendation for mercy. The lieutenant governor considered the recommendation for mercy in both cases, but the death sentence was allowed to stand.

Wait's young wife Maria, who was about twenty, and Chandler's eldest daughter Sarah, eighteen, immediately decided to travel to Quebec to see the Earl of Durham. The two had a difficult time even getting an audience with Lord Durham, but they persisted doggedly. Lord Durham finally saw them and wrote a letter of clemency. They took the letter to Lieutenant Governor George Arthur, who at first refused to accede to clemency, saying, "I cannot accede to this request and prevent the due course of the law upon offences of this nature." But Maria threatened to return to Lord Durham and Arthur acquiesced, though he tried to stall getting word to the jail. With the executions set for October 30, word came down on October 29 to the jail that both men would be spared and given life in "one of Her Majesty's penal colonies."

Both Wait and his wife Maria kept extensive journals of these occurrences, which Maria called a tale of "thrilling sorrow, misery and woe." The two prisoners, along with others all in hand and foot shackles, were taken to Kingston and Fort Henry. Maria followed and visited her husband once before they were transferred to Quebec. Maria returned to Niagara to pick up her daughter, Augusta, and then went to Lockport to stay with friends.

The journey across the Atlantic took twenty-five days in, as Wait put it, "abject misery." The prisoners were not allowed out of the hold and only two buckets sufficed for toilets. The food consisted of hard black biscuits, gruel and meat "that was nearly putrid." Wait added that the conditions "were too revolting to be described."

Maria, who refused to give up on her husband, traveled to London to beg for a pardon from the queen. Maria wrote in her journal, "The queen expressed herself as being much touched by the circumstances of the case and was pleased to say that she would consult her ministers." But nothing came of this entreaty, so Maria returned home while Wait and Chandler, along with other prisoners, were shipped to the penal colony at Van Diemen's Land, an island off the southern coast of Australia. The journey took four months.

It was an unpleasant trip. Wait wrote, "Surely, if there are places in human abodes deserving the title of Hell, one is a transport ship, crowded with felons, culled from England's most abandoned criminals." They arrived at Van Diemen's Land on July 18, 1839. While the English penal colony was no picnic, the prisoners fared better than they had on the transport ships or in the temporary jails that housed them during the long journey. And it was far better than the conditions at the French penal colony of Devil's Island.

After landing, the prisoners were marched to the Hobart Penitentiary where the governor, Sir John Franklin, explained the terms of their imprisonment. The terms seemed quite lenient compared with the wretched condition in jails and prison transport ships. The prisoners were given a probationary period in which they were allowed to leave prison during the day, assigned to "masters" on the island where they would work for free. After a satisfactory probation period, prisoners were issued a "ticket" that allowed them to seek their own masters and work for slight pay.

Eventually, Samuel Chandler and Benjamin Wait were assigned to a six-thousand-acre estate about fifty miles north of the Hobart Prison. Chandler worked as a carpenter and Wait as a clerk and storekeeper. The workday, Wait wrote in his journal, began at 4:00 a.m. and lasted until 11:00 p.m. When they were off work, the ticket allowed them to roam the island. This presented the opportunity for escape when the men learned several American ships were at the Hobart harbor.

In December 1841 Chandler obtained a ten-day pass and went to the harbor where he met a fellow Mason and captain of one of the American whaling ships. They made their escape plans. Chandler and Wait could not board the ship in the harbor because it was thoroughly searched before it left. They obtained a rowboat under the pretext of going fishing and rowed laboriously out well past the harbor. They were in the boat, with little food and water, for several days and were about to return to the island when they spotted the whaler and were taken aboard.

The men were on the first leg of the road to freedom, but they were still thousands of miles and seven months away from home. They took tasks helping the crew catch whales on the journey. Unfortunately, the whaler hit a violent storm off the coast of South America and was wrecked near Brazil. Wait and Chandler soon found themselves penniless, but glad to be alive, in Rio de Janeiro.

They met a captain from Bristol, Rhode Island, who was going back to New York. He agreed to take the passengers with payment promised at a future date. Canadian historian Colin K. Duquemin wrote, "On arrival in New York, Freemasons extended the hand of friendship to Chandler and by association to Wait. They mustered up funds to buy train tickets for the two men."

The pair traveled to Niagara Falls where Wait's wife Maria was working as a teacher. About the reunion with his wife, Wait wrote, "Over the circumstances of our meeting I will draw the curtain of silence and leave the fancy of the reader to portray it."

Chandler and Wait would not return to Canada, of course, because the treason convictions remained against them. Maria died on May 31, 1843, during childbirth. Wait moved to Elmira where he worked as a barrel maker.

Wait continued to take a deep interest in Canada's move toward democracy, but he was "upset that his contribution and that of his fellow Patriots had not been sufficiently recognized." Wait moved to Michigan, where he died on November 9, 1895.

Samuel Chandler, his wife Ann and their children moved to Iowa, where his eldest daughter Sarah and her husband lived. Upon Chandler's death, William Lyon Mackenzie wrote, "a more trusty, faithful, brotherly minded man I have never met with."

Mackenzie had served a short term in a Rochester jail for violating U.S. neutrality laws. He was later pardoned in Canada and returned to Toronto where he was elected to the assembly serving from 1850–58. He died in Toronto in August of 1861.

# PART III

# Significant People

# Winfield Scott

One of America's greatest military leaders, Winfield Scott, (like the old soldier who never dies) has faded unceremoniously into history. But at one time, he had strong ties to Niagara County. Scott (1786–1866) had an inauspicious start in the military, but he came into prominence right here in western New York State because of his brave fighting in the War of 1812.

Scott visited Niagara County frequently to see his many friends, including Major Bonajah Mallory in Lockport and, in Niagara Falls, Peter B. Porter and Parkhurst Whitney, owner of the Eagle Tavern and later the famed Cataract House. Scott also stared down the British and prevented a third conflict with England in helping to end the Patriots' War.

Born near Petersburg, Virginia, on June 13, 1786, he attended the College of William and Mary and became a lawyer. He joined the army in 1807 as a commissioned officer. While serving in New Orleans in 1809 he called his commander, General James Wilkinson, "a traitor, liar and scoundrel."

Scott was court-martialed and given a one-year suspension from active duty. He twice thought seriously about returning to the practice of law, but then the War of 1812 broke out and, as a lieutenant colonel, he led troops into combat at the battle of Queenston Heights. He was captured and held for three months before being returned in a prisoner exchange.

In May 1813 Scott led the amphibious assault on Fort George; he captured the fort but was wounded. After recovering, he was promoted to brigadier general and, in March 1814, he led troops in the battles of Chippewa and Lundy's Lane, where he was again wounded.

Scott recognized that, in that war, the state militia lacked military discipline. In fact, militia troops refused to go to the aid of their comrades, who were being slaughtered in the battle of Queenston Heights, because they were state troops and could not be ordered out of the country.

A statue of an eagle was used to mark the old Eagle Tavern. The eagle is now in the Local History Department of the Niagara Falls Public Library. *Photo courtesy of the Local History Department.*

Before the 1814 invasion of Canada, Scott initiated a rigorous training program emphasizing repeated drills and strict adherence to military dress and manners. He became known among the troops as "Old Fuss and Feathers," but he turned the militia into a superb combat team. By the end of the war, he was promoted to major general and became well respected among the military and a folk hero to the civilian population.

Scott brought professionalism to the military by writing the army's first drill book, borrowing from the French manual of arms. On July 5, 1841, Scott was named to head the entire U.S. military, a position he held for the next twenty years, longer than any top general in history.

General Scott also became a good negotiator. He negotiated a treaty avoiding war with the Sauk and Fox Indians in 1838, and in 1839 he settled border disputes between Canada and the New England states, averting a threatened conflict with England. He did the same in the Patriots' War when Canadian dissidents and United States friends occupied Canadian Navy Island in preparation for a war of liberation in Canada in 1837. Scott acquired a ship and moved the troops off Navy Island. A British ship threatened to fire on Scott's ship and he was fully prepared to retaliate, but the British blinked. No shots were exchanged and war was again averted.

Scott returned to this area in peacetime to visit friends and to speak to a friendly crowd at the American Hotel in Lockport. During the Mexican War, Scott, perhaps recalling his success in capturing Fort George, led a major amphibious assault at Vera Cruz, defeated General Santa Anna and became military governor of Mexico. After returning to Washington, he became involved in politics and decided to seek the presidency. He failed to gain the Whig party nomination in 1848 but garnered the nomination four years later and, despite his wartime popularity, was soundly defeated by Franklin Pierce.

At the outbreak of the Civil War, Scott had served in the military for a half century and was too old to actively participate. He urged Lincoln to select Robert E. Lee to head the army, but Lee opted to fight for the South. Both Lee and Ulysses S. Grant had served under Scott as junior officers.

Scott retired on November 1, 1861, but he lived to see his battle plan for the Civil War adopted by Lincoln and Grant and it proved successful. He died at West Point in May 1866, just days before his eightieth birthday.

# Nellie Bly on the Great John L.

The great woman journalist Nellie Bly put a different and somewhat feminine spin on the Great John L. Sullivan's training in nearby Belfast, New York, for the Kilrain fight. Sullivan, who had put on exhibitions in Lockport and Niagara Falls, chafed under the training regimens of William Muldoon at Muldoon's home in Belfast. He slipped out one night to a nearby saloon, but was retrieved by Muldoon before much damage could be done. Bly, during interviews with Sullivan, was given a much different perspective.

Nellie Bly, whose real name was Elizabeth Cochrane Seaman, interviewed Sullivan at Muldoon's and wrote a Sunday feature painting more of a rosy picture of the champ in training for the heavyweight title fight with Jake Kilrain in Richburg, Mississippi.

Sullivan won in seventy-five rounds, the last title fight under the London Prize ring rules for bare-knuckle fighting. Rochester's Henry W. Clune wrote that Sullivan's training regimen was anything but smooth.

Bly's piece appeared in the *New York World* on Sunday, May 26, 1889. With a woman's touch, she described Muldoon's house "in the prettiest part of town" as "a very pretty little two story building surrounded by the smoothest and greenest of green lawns."

When she first met Sullivan, she saw "a tall man with enormous shoulders" who was wearing "dark trousers, a light cheviot coat and vest and slippers." She asked him what he wore for his walks and runs and he said he wore a sweater. Apparently that was a fairly new piece of apparel that Nellie Bly had never heard of so Sullivan brought one out and showed it to her.

The training seemed to agree with him. He said he was losing weight: "When I came here I weighed 237 pounds and now I weigh 218. Before I leave here I will weigh only 195 pounds."

Bly also inquired about his diet. He said, "I eat nothing fattening. I have oatmeal for breakfast and meat and bread for dinner and cold meat and stale bread for supper. I eat no sweets nor potatoes. I used to smoke all day but since I came here I haven't seen a cigar. Occasionally Mr. Muldoon gives me a glass of ale, but it doesn't average one a day."

Sullivan was notorious for his prodigious drinking, but Nellie Bly did not question that aspect of his life. She did query, however, "Then training is not very pleasant work?"

Sullivan replied, "It's the worst thing going. A fellow would rather fight twelve dozen times than train one, but it's got to be done."

He said after breakfast he and Muldoon would go for a twelve-mile walk and run that took about two hours. "In the afternoon," he said, "we wrestle, punch a bag, throw football, swing Indian clubs and dumbbells, practice the chest movement and such things until suppertime."

"Do you like prizefighting?" Bly asked.

"I don't," Sullivan replied. "Of course I did once, or rather I was fond of traveling about and the excitement of the crowds, but this is my last fight."

"What will you do if you stop fighting?" she asked.

"If I win this fight I will travel for a year giving sparring exhibitions, and then I will settle down. I have always wanted to run a hotel in New York and if I am successful, I think I shall spend the rest of my life as a hotel proprietor."

"How much money have you made during your career as a prize fighter?"

"I have made $500,000 or $600,000 in boxing. I made $125,000 from September 26, 1883, to May 26, 1884, when I traveled through the country offering $1,000 to anyone I couldn't knock out in four rounds, which takes twelve minutes."

The Great John L. Sullivan, according to pioneer investigative journalist Bly, began prizefighting at age nineteen when he decided to take on a man who had never been knocked down. Sullivan expounded, "I had a match with a prize man who had never been downed and I was the winner. This got me lots of notice so I went through the country giving exhibitions."

He said he wore spiked shoes when fighting to prevent slipping.

Bly asked, "How will you fight Kilrain, with or without gloves?"

Sullivan replied, "I will fight Kilrain according to the London Prize ring rules. That's without gloves and allows wrestling and throwing a man down." Jack Broughton published the first boxing rules in 1743. He was recognized as the third heavyweight champion of the world.

Sullivan also explained to Bly the fairly new Marquis of Queensberry Rules published by John Graham Chambers in 1865. Chambers was sponsored by John Sholto Douglas, the eighth Marquis of Queensberry, who lent his name to the rules but did not draft them.

Sullivan said, "Under the Marquis of Queensberry Rules, we wear gloves, anything under eleven ounces. They give us three minutes to a round under the Queensberry and when the three minutes are up, you have to rest whether you could whip your man the next instant or not."

Bly asked to examine his hands, which she termed "very soft and small for a fighter." She described them thus: "The fingers were straight and shapely.

The closely trimmed nails were lovely oval and pink. The only apparent difference was the great thickness through."

She also felt his bicep, which was "like a rock. With both my hands I tried to span it, but I couldn't. Meanwhile the great fellow sat there watching me with a most boyish expression of amusement."

Sullivan said he rinsed his face and hands with a concoction of "rock salt and white wine and vinegar and several other ingredients" to toughen the skin.

Then, the following exchange occurred:

> *"Do you hit a man on the face and neck and anywhere you can?"* [Bly] *asked.*
>
> *"Certainly, any place above the belt that I get a chance,"* *and he smiled.*
>
> *"Don't you hate to hit a man so?"*
>
> *"I don't think about it,"* *still smiling.*
>
> *"When you see that you have hurt him, don't you feel sorry?"*
>
> *"I never feel sorry until the fight is over."*
>
> *"How do you feel when you get hit very hard?"*
>
> *The dark, bright eyes glanced at* [Bly] *lazily and the deep, deep voice said with feeling:* *"I only want a chance to hit back."*

Nellie Bly had lunch with Sullivan and Mr. and Mrs. Muldoon, as well as the trainers. She was impressed with the surroundings, including "the white table linen and beautiful dishes, down to the large bunch of fragrant lilacs and another of beautifully shaped and colored wild flowers, separated by a slipper filled with velvety pansies [which were] all entirely foreign to any idea [she] had ever conceived of prize fighters and their surroundings."

Muldoon praised his charge by telling Bly, "Mr. Sullivan is the most obedient man I ever saw. He hasn't asked for a drink or a smoke since he came here and takes what I allow him without a murmur. It is a pleasure to train him."

Sullivan told Bly, "You are the first woman who ever interviewed me and I have given you more than I ever gave any reporter in my life. They generally manufacture things and credit them to me, although some are mighty good fellows."

Bly ended her story: "And then the carriage came to take us to the train, and after I bade them all goodbye I shook hands with John L. Sullivan and wished him success in the coming fight, and I believe he will have it too, don't you?"

# Lewis Payne

North Tonawanda, known for lumber production and shipbuilding in earlier times, had a somewhat lesser renown in contributing to various war efforts. One of the heroes of the Civil War was North Tonawanda's Colonel Lewis S. Payne. He also made a mark as a Niagara County politician.

In the not too distant history, North Tonawanda utilized its shipbuilding ability to aid the nation during World War II. The Bison Boat Company, located on Tonawanda Island, built landing barges for the navy during the war. Naval landing barges played a critical part in the war effort by placing fighting men on the shores of many a Pacific Island. Landing barges also played a prominent role in the war in Europe, most notably during "The Longest Day," or the invasion of Nazi-occupied France across the English Channel.

There were undoubtedly many North Tonawanda youths who performed heroically in the various wars over the years. But one of the best known was Colonel Payne, for whom Payne Avenue was named. He settled in North Tonawanda in 1841 and built the first steam-operated saw mill to speed the cutting and trimming of logs into lumber. He started a large wheat-growing farm in 1847 at the corner of Wheatfield Street and Payne Avenue.

Aside from his farming and business interests, he dabbled in politics and served as a supervisor, collector of canal tolls and as county clerk. When the Civil War broke out in 1861, President Lincoln immediately put out a call for seventy-five thousand volunteers. Payne answered the patriotic call and, at his own expense, raised an infantry company of volunteers from around the county. He became captain of the company, which became part of the Hundredth Regiment of Infantry.

The company participated in many of the famous battles of the Civil War. Payne distinguished himself for his bravery and knowledge of military combat tactics. One commando excursion led by Captain Payne occurred on a dark night at Charleston Harbor. The company was given the task of rowing boats into the harbor under cover of darkness and destroying a Confederate steamer. The flames attracted the attention of onshore Rebel artillerymen and the battery opened fire on Captain Payne's company.

The men were rowing desperately back to the Union shore when a typical military snafu occurred. Payne's soldiers felt some relief when they finally rowed out of range of the enemy cannon. But, unfortunately, Union guards had not been informed of the Union night raid into the harbor and they began

Civil War cannon now located in Porter Park in Niagara Falls.

unloading "friendly fire" from their positions in the woods upon Captain Payne and his men landing on shore. Captain Payne quickly pulled out his huge white handkerchief and began waving it frantically. The guards were fearful of a Confederate trick, but they held up their fire and approached cautiously until they could confirm that it was Union soldiers they were firing upon. Luckily, there were no casualties.

Payne was soon promoted to colonel. In 1862, he was wounded in a skirmish and captured by the Rebels. He recovered from his wounds, but spent three years in a Rebel prison camp. Because each side in the Civil War had trouble attracting volunteers as the war dragged on, and because they were running out of space and supplies to hold and care for prisoners, periodic exchanges of prisoners were agreed upon. Payne was returned during such a prisoner exchange in 1865.

Colonel Payne was prominently mentioned in a popular national publication of 1867, *Harper's Magazine*, in an article entitled "Heroic Deeds of Heroic Men." Upon his return to North Tonawanda in 1865, he became county clerk again. In 1869 he was elected to the New York State Assembly and then, in 1877, he was elected state senator.

During the Civil War, many residents feared that England would join the South and there was the distinct threat that English and Canadian forces would invade Niagara County across the border. President Lincoln favored deepening the Erie Canal so that the larger gunboats could be sent throughout the Great Lakes, but neither Congress nor New York State would fund the project.

However, even after the Civil War, there were lingering fears of the unprotected border to Canada. The U.S. Navy Department decided to build a gunboat at North Tonawanda. The *Lockport Journal* of August 28, 1861, carried an article that stated, "It is not known to our readers generally that Uncle Sam is building a first class gunboat near the junction of the Tonawanda Creek and the Niagara River." The article said the boat was nearly ready for a trial run. The boat was 175 feet long and 57 feet wide with a beam of 11 feet. The cost of boat construction was set at $175,000. The crew included forty men and nine officers, and there were six guns broadside. The article added, "The boat will be a valuable accession to the means of defense on the lakes in the event, which we trust is far distant, of a war with Great Britain."

The reporter continued, "Through the courtesy of the gentlemanly canal collector at that place, we were introduced to the builder, James D. Leary, a very affable and intelligent gentleman, and the veteran captain of the boat, Captain Martin, of the U.S. Navy."

# Jimmy Duffy

The presence of the Great John L. Sullivan in Lockport and Niagara Falls in the early part of the last century brings to mind the many local boxers who made it big in the world's toughest sport. Both Lockport and Niagara Falls, as well as nearby Buffalo and environs (witness Baby Joe Mesi's rise to fame), have produced fighters worthy of note. But one standout among the lower-weight fighters sprang from the mean streets of Lockport in the early 1900s. He was the redoubtable Jimmy Duffy.

Jimmy Duffy was one of Lockport's contributions to the all-time greats of the fight world. Born in 1889 on Gooding Street, the affable Irishman graced the same ring with such greats as Benny Leonard, Packy McFarland, Freddie

Professional boxer Jimmy Duffy was from Lockport, New York. He was the best fighter in his day.

Welsh and Rocky Kansas, among others. For Jimmy there were many such glory—and gory—days.

There was the night of July 3, 1912, when Jimmy met Knockout Brown in Buffalo—one of his first big fights. Brown was fresh from a draw with the then current champion Ad Wolgast. But Jimmy took his measure and won impressively in ten rounds.

In that year, Jimmy, who first laced on his tools of trade at the age of twelve, fought some of the best lightweights in the country. He met the English champion Freddie Welsh, Leach Cross, young Jack O'Brien and Packy McFarland. Newspaper accounts credit Jimmy with wins or draws in all of these fights.

Jimmy showed a lot of "heart" on May 29, 1913, in the old Broadway auditorium in Buffalo. That night, he squared off with Jack Britton, who had met and beaten just about everybody around. Near the end of the third round, Britton unleashed a right hook that dropped Jimmy like a shot. But the Lockport warrior made it to his feet by the count of nine and managed to weather the round. From that point on, the fight turned into a corking slugfest. However, in the sixth round, Britton threw a low blow and the referee awarded the fight to Jimmy. In all, Jimmy fought Britton five times. Later, Britton was to win the welterweight championship, which he subsequently lost to the "Toy Bulldog," Mickey Walker.

The title seemed to elude Jimmy. His closest encounter with it, perhaps, could be seen in his bouts with Freddie Welsh. In their second match at Saint Louis in 1914, Jimmy decked the scrappy native of Wales in the fifth round and went on to win by a substantial margin, according to newspaper accounts. Just five months later, Welsh won the world crown from Willie Richie. When Jimmy met Welsh the third time in Buffalo, Welsh insisted they come in over the lightweight limit so he would not lose his title if Jimmy beat him. This turned out to be a wise move on the part of Welsh. Four of the five newspapers credited Jimmy with the win; the fifth called it a draw.

During the decade Jimmy fought, he took on no less than six world champions: Jack Britton, Benny Leonard, Ted Lewis, Freddie Welsh, Johnny Dundee and Rocky Kansas. In the fight world, this was keeping fast company no matter how you looked at it.

After his fight with Dundee, a United Press account had this to say: "Johnny Dundee would have had a chance with Jimmy Duffy last night if the latter had consented to have his left arm strapped to his side." After Jimmy's second fight with Welsh, another great champion, Ad Wolgast, had only praise for the Lockport boy. Wolgast said, "I'll be honest with you and say that Duffy is about the best in the game."

In the summer of 1915, at the height of his career, Jimmy suffered an unfortunate setback. He was in an automobile accident, which for a time threatened to end his fighting days. His leg was so badly injured that amputation was considered. But plucky Jimmy did come back. By winter, he once again was ready to climb through the ropes. However, the injury had taken its toll and nudged Jimmy over his peak. He never again seemed to recover his old form.

Nevertheless, there were still some good fights left in him. In November, he traveled to Boston to square off with Ted Lewis. Early in the fight, Lewis, a thunderous puncher, put Jimmy down for a nine count; although he was able to get up, his mind never cleared. Before the fight was over Jimmy hit the canvas seven more times. Each time his game heart brought him to his feet, but only to face a losing cause. After that, Jimmy lost to the immortal Benny Leonard in Tulsa. And, when Rocky Kansas scored a knockout, Jimmy knew his boxing days were over and he hung up his gloves for good.

Bert Finch, who was once Jimmy's manager, called Jimmy "the best fighter I ever saw, pound for pound." Describing Jimmy's prowess, he commented, "He could nearly break your neck with his short, cutting left jab and he could take you out with his right cross, a punch that rarely traveled over 10 inches."

After retirement, Jimmy became a Niagara County sheriff's deputy and served with distinction for twenty-seven years. He made a good cop as well as a good fighter. In the late 1950s, Jimmy's wife, Alice Duffy, was elected a supervisor from Lockport's First Ward.

Jimmy was inducted into the Hall of Fame at the Sixth Annual Banquet of the Buffalo Veteran Boxers Association on August 9, 2002.

# King Camp Gillette

Although not a fighter, another scrappy man wanted to bring renown to the Niagara area. King Camp Gillette was a struggling salesman and a not-very-creative inventor until he was forty years old, when he had a revelation while staring into his mirror and shaving with a straight razor. But before he invented the safety razor on his way to becoming a millionaire, he wrote an imaginative book about creating a utopia around Niagara Falls. Because of the tremendous power of Niagara Falls, Gillette believed this area should become the center of the economic universe. In his book, he wrote:

> *For many reasons I have come to the conclusion that there is no spot on the American continent, or possibly in the world, that combines so many natural advantages as that section of our country lying in the vicinity of the Niagara Falls, extending east into New York State and west into Ontario.*

He called this great new Utopian city "Metropolis" and envisioned it stretching from Rochester to Hamilton. He pictured sixty million people living in thousands of twenty-five-story cylindrical apartment buildings.

When he got into the economic flow of capitalism with his invention, he concentrated on making millions for his own family and forgot about his utopia, except for the one he created for himself. He never even opened a razor factory in Niagara Falls. But then, there were no IDAs (Industrial Development Agencies) at the time to give him tax breaks.

# Misery of Elijah Smith

Elijah Smith wasn't born under a dark cloud of gloom and doom on Friday the thirteenth after his mother passed a black cat and ducked under a ladder. But he might as well have been, according to the journal of his life in nineteenth-century Niagara County. Elijah Smith's life, despite numerous opportunities for wealth and happiness, dissolved into a series of improbable misfortunes. The sad story of this sad sack was recounted by the late county historian Clarence O. Lewis in 1957 after he located Smith's handwritten journal in archives at Cornell University.

Smith's bad luck began in 1803 when he settled in the Mohawk Valley with his wife. He wrote, "I built a [frame] house and [dug] a well and in 1809 we found our title was good for nothing so I lost my little home."

Smith moved to Scipio to practice his trade of carpentry, and then he decided to buy land near Lewiston from the Holland Land Company in 1816. He obtained carpentry jobs across the river in Queenston and mailed seventy dollars cash to his wife so she and their five children could join him. The money was lost. He wrote, "I made some search for it but all in vain so I wrote again to have her come and I would pay the fare when they arrived and so they did."

Things were looking up for the family. They settled about nine miles from Lewiston where he "built [them] a good log house on the Mountain Ridge Road" on 120 acres, for which he paid $200 down from his earnings in Canada. He paid $4.50 an acre and had eight years (the first two interest free) to pay off the mortgage. Smith wrote, "At this time we were all well and I could see nothing to hinder me from getting rich, but the hand of Providence had determined otherwise." Within two years Smith was "rejected off the land and lost every cent of [his] layout and all [he] had paid." This happened after he found himself strapped for a little cash and asked a man living nearby to lend him $65, for which he handed over his Holland Land Company article, or deed, for collateral. Smith agreed to pay it back in six months. Again, all seemed well. But his luck did not last.

Another neighbor, hearing of the transaction, warned Smith he was dealing with a scoundrel and that his "farm is gone." Smith became concerned, got the money in three months and went to the county clerk's office in Lewiston, but the other man had been there previously and had registered the deed in his own name. Smith wrote, "I came home with a heavy heart. The next morning I went to him with the money but he would not touch it, but told me I must leave the farm immediately or he would put me out."

Then he made a deal for twenty-five acres, cleared trees, built another log cabin and got carpentry work in Canada to pay for it. He hired a man for $25 to clear more trees and fence the land while he was away working, and Smith also gave him $10 for seed. When he returned, he found the man had gone with his oxen and chains and learned "he had sold [Smith's] oxen and chains which cost [him] over $130. Here was $165 gone in cash which [Smith] had labored hard for." He hired lawyers to try to recoup some of the loss and he did manage to get his oxen back from the man who had bought them. However, about the oxen he wrote, "I might as well let them alone for I had to pay the lawyers all they were worth."

At one point in his diary Smith commiserated, "I was surrounded by losses, crosses and disappointments." And it wasn't over yet. Even a planned peaceful fishing trip in the spring turned disastrous.

It was a fine March day when Elijah Smith decided to take his two oldest sons on an overnight fishing trip to Tonawanda Creek about eight miles from his (as yet) unfinished log cabin at Upper Mountain and Thrall Roads. Even with this pleasant diversion, bad luck dogged Elijah Smith's every step. It was as if he couldn't move without that dark cloud hovering over his head.

In his life's journal, which detailed all the misery, Smith wrote that he and his two oldest boys trekked through thick and uninhabited forestland, two miles of it a swamp, to Tonawanda Creek. The fishing was good in those days but, like today, the March weather was quite unpredictable. Smith wrote, "Soon after we arrived at the creek, it began to rain and continued all that day and night, toward morning it turned into snow which fell three or four inches deep and the creek was swelling over its banks and quite muddy and we [were] obliged to give up fishing."

Smith went to a nearby Dutch settlement to ask about the best route home and he was told to take the high ground of Bear Ridge, but he still had to traverse the swamp. Smith had talked to Jacob Crisman and Martin Van Slyke, who settled there in 1807. Smith and his boys found the ridge but the swamp was another matter. It was, he said, "like a sea" with the water up to his thighs. He and his boys, ages twelve and fourteen, waded carefully through the water for two miles, feeling with their feet for sunken logs and other debris. Smith wrote, "My youngest boy got so benumbed before we got through I had to take him on my back for it was the month of March and the water was cold." When they finally got through the swamp, Smith got lost in the woods about two miles from his home. Luckily, he ran into some neighbors who took him to their home about a half mile from his unfinished cabin.

Still another blow awaited him. Smith's neighbor had some bad news:

> *Your house is all burnt to ashes, said he. Oh, I said, do not try to make me feel any worse for I am almost dead now. It is true, said he. By this time my wife came to the door and said it is true our house is all burnt to ashes and everything in it and we scattered all over the neighborhood. At this time we had nine children.*

In a supreme understatement, Smith wrote, "I was almost discouraged but I found it would not do to give up."

The next month, April of 1818, Smith gave up his twenty-five acres and moved a mile east to "squat" on "100 acres of wild land for which I was not able to get an article (deed)." With the help of friends, he put up yet another log cabin, cleared an acre for a vegetable crop and then put in wheat and corn. It was so shaded by the thick forest, he said, that the crops did not amount to much and the large family ran out of food by April of the next year. Smith wrote, "I set out in pursuit of something to eat, leaving my family with nothing to eat but a peck of potatoes."

He walked to Niagara Falls, Lewiston and Youngstown, and then

> *about 18 miles east on the Ridge but I returned home without a morsel. My children flocked around me asking if I brought them something to eat. This was cutting to my very heart. It was May 1819. I sat with my head in my hands saying to my wife I have done all I can do and I don't know what will become of us.*

Smith's wife told him "the Lord will provide for us." Not fifteen minutes later, he wrote:

> *One of my neighbors came in by the name of Vaughn Weaver and said to me Mr. Smith I have just come from Nathan Comstock and he told me if you would come and see him and bring your tools and work for him he would let you have something to eat.*

Nathan Comstock, a prominent Quaker, had settled in Lockport in 1816 and he occupied a large farm where the Odd Fellows Home is now located.

Hard luck Elijah Smith managed to land a job doing carpentry work for Comstock on his farm in 1819. He desperately needed food to feed his starving family. Comstock asked him if he had any food to last until he got paid and, in his journal, Smith wrote, "Not a thing, said I. So he gave me some pork and Indian meal." When he got home with the provisions, it was after dark and the family was in bed "but," he wrote, "my wife arose and went to cooking. I called the children and we had a good feast that night."

His job and the food it provided lasted until he harvested his crops and "we fared well enough, but as yet we had no cow. I agreed with a neighbor to chop five acres of timber for a cow." Now things were really looking up, but Mother Nature once again intervened. He explained, "About one week after I got her I returned one night from Lewiston and saw my cow very stupid and not willing to eat. I got her to the house, but about 9 o'clock in the evening

I found her stone dead." It seems a limb broke off a tree and broke a blood vessel in the cow's head. Even with the cow dead, he had to complete cutting timber on the neighbor's five acres until his debt was paid.

In the spring of 1821, Smith was able to land a carpentry job in Lockport building the Erie Canal and the locks. There was a lot of traffic by his house consisting of men from Canada seeking work on the canal, so he had his wife start up "a little cake and bean shop." Then he decided to start a tavern business at his home to sell hard liquor. This, he said, lasted eight years. He was offered $500 for his farm so he decided to take it and, with his savings, he bought 360 acres about a mile and a half south of his home.

He returned home after viewing this new site and his girls were making supper while his wife was "in the bed with a sick headache." When supper was ready, they could not find his little boy Daniel. Smith wrote,

> *I looked into the well and behold there he lay floating on top of the water on his left side partly circled up. The well was about eight feet deep and almost full. Not more than two breaths before we were rejoicing about our new home and now we were mourning the loss of our six-year-old son. After this trouble, I concluded to give up the idea of a new farm and stay where I was so I went on with my little tavern.*

The inherent danger of a tavern business soon overcame him—just another plank in the flooring of his bad luck. "Soon after I opened the tavern," he wrote, "I was so impudent and unfortunate as to sup a little myself and the longer I kept the more I supped until I got an idea I could not very well do without it." He drank heavily for several years, "until," he said, "I began to think my family were all against me. This created a coolness and indifference in me toward my family but I still continued to sup." In addition, he neglected his farm work and the peacefulness of his family "was broken up." Smith added, "Still the devil told me I had better keep right on and not mind my family. If I did they would get me under their thumb." His wife gathered up the children and left him.

It then struck him that he had to return to religion to turn his life around. Elijah Smith, in an effort to turn around his life, which had been filled with bad luck, dropped down on his knees in the woods one day and asked God for help. In his journal, he wrote that he realized his wife and family had not left him "but that I had left them by supping that accursed liquor and that they were praying for me." Smith said, "I here formed a resolution to let liquor alone with the exception of a good drink three times a day just before eating."

Smith also noted that excessive drinking was killing him. He wrote:

> *I was about 48 years old, right in the bloom of life and now while I am writing these lines I am 78 years old and the remainder of my life is hid from me but it must be short. So here is 30 years added to my life, I believe, by abstaining from that poisonous cup.*

His family returned. His farm and business improved. But he found that even cutting down on his drinking wasn't enough.

> *I concluded then not to touch a drop of liquor at home but if I went to Lockport I would take a drink with my friends. I soon found every time I went to Lockport and took one or two drinks it was sure to give me a headache. So I made up my mind not to meddle with the accursed liquor at all and joined the temperance pledge.*

In 1831, he said, he sold the tavern and bought a fifty-five-acre farm nearby with a frame house on it. His children either died or moved off and, in 1834, his wife took sick and died. Smith said, "I was now alone, except for my aged mother who was helpless, so I concluded to get another wife, but it was an unfortunate job for me as you will soon hear."

He found a widow who had eight children, two of them still living with her, and married her on December 5, 1838. They moved into his house and all "lived in peace and harmony until spring." He said his new wife "would often say that she had a good many offers to get married but she had waited long enough and now had a good pious husband but she soon altered her mind."

Soon dissension set in. "About the first of March," he wrote, "I discovered an uneasiness." One morning, he was called to breakfast and, he wrote, "I took my Bible in hand to read a chapter as my practice was," but his wife stopped him saying, "Mr. Smith we will omit reading and praying this morning." He complied, but the same thing happened the next morning and "I told her it was my duty to my God and therefore I could not omit it and so I took my Bible and sat down to read." His wife and her two daughters left the table and went into the living room "and while I was reading and trying to pray they kept a continual groaning and saying glory amen too loud." Smith added, "From that time on she opposed me in everything of a religious nature and declared she did not believe there was anything in religion so I went it alone until April 4 when I was gone to town meeting."

When he returned, the house was dark, so he made his way to the bed when, to his surprise, "she said to me Mr. Smith, you cannot sleep here tonight." He then "lit a candle and found her goods all packed up and a good many of my own with them." She told him she was leaving him first thing in the morning.

And so, old Elijah Smith, after a lifetime of sorrow, was left all alone again. His travails hopefully ended with his death in 1858.

# PART IV

# *Significant Places*

# Scow Rescue

One of the most dramatic rescues, which left behind a tourist curiosity, happened in the upper Niagara River between Goat Island and the Canadian shore about a thousand yards from the brink of the Horseshoe Falls. The accident left the hulk of an old steel scow sitting in the swift current that for years baffled many a tourist who wandered out to the end of the Three Sisters Islands off the southeast corner of Goat Island.

The incident began on the afternoon of August 6, 1918, when a tugboat pulling the scow went aground near the entrance to the old Hydraulic Canal a short distance east of the falls. Two other tugboats were dispatched to pull the tug and scow free from the rocks. But, in attempting to push the tug free, the other two boats sheared off the towline to the scow, setting it adrift in the treacherous upper rapids. The two workers onboard the scow, which had no power of its own, were James H. Harris and Gustave F. Lofberg, both of Buffalo. When they realized their danger, they began punching holes in the bottom of the scow in an attempt to scuttle it before it went over the brink and carried them to certain death. They also threw an anchor overboard and, fortunately, it finally became snared on the rocks, halting the scow's inexorable march to the brink.

As news of the impending disaster spread, hundreds of spectators lined the shore to watch the drama unfold. Rescuers decided to try to get a "breeches buoy" out to the scuttled scow and obtained the cable and recruits from the army post at Fort Niagara and the U.S. Lifesaving Station at Youngstown. A breeches buoy was a basket-type contraption attached to the cable and pulled along the cable by heavy ropes. Rescuers hoped to fasten the cable between the scow and the Canadian shore and then pull the men in the basket to safety. A cannon set up on the roof of the Canadian Hydroelectric Power Building was used to fire one end of the cable to the scow. This worked well, and the two men onboard fastened the cable securely to the scow and the cable was winched tight. The basket was then pulled by rope along the cable over the raging current toward the scow.

A real snag developed when the rope pulling the basket became ensnarled with the cable and the basket could not reach the scow. Night was rapidly approaching and searchlights were set up on shore to continue rescue efforts. Veteran Canadian river man William "Red" Hill Sr. appeared on the scene and volunteered to ride the basket out to the snarl and untangle the rope so the basket could continue to the scow. Hill's first trip over the rapids came at 3:00 a.m. and nearly ended in tragedy as the cable sagged, dropping the basket into the raging waters. Hill hung on but was forced to return to shore.

However, after a few more hours rescuers were able to winch the cable tight again and the river man, on his second trip at about 9:30 a.m. was able to untangle the ropes. The basket was hauled to the scow and the men, one at a time, were pulled safely to shore.

Everyone expected the scow to be swept over the falls before much longer. But, despite the treacherous current there, the scow remained lodged on the rocks for years, itself becoming a sort of tourist attraction. The relentless current washed part of the scow over the Horseshoe Falls in October 1947, but a small part of the scow hull still remains. It is barely visible from the American Three Sisters Island, but it makes a fine roost for the seagulls.

# Ice Bridge Tragedy

Niagara's celebrated ice bridge, that frozen tundra below the falls stretching from the United States to Canada, brought an emotion-packed, spine-tingling death in 1912. Mother Nature can be beautiful as well as cruel, as she was on a bright but cold February 4, 1912. She brought an unexpectedly sudden, but tortuously lingering, death to a Cleveland youth and a Toronto couple. She alternately brought hope and despair: there were cheers and wails of grief from the hundreds of spectators who had flocked to the gorge to witness the human drama.

Niagara Falls is well known for its summer splendor. But each winter, during January and February, the normally chilling temperatures bring a winter wonderland scene to the falls. Now, visitors can only look at the ice

The ice bridge formed below the falls in 1875. Vending stands were set up to accommodate tourists walking on the ice.

bridge, which an 1841 guidebook described as "splendours surpassing those of the Polar Seas." Today, people are banned from venturing out on the ice bridge, but it was not always so.

At one time, before the tragedy, tourists were encouraged to walk out on the ice bridge. Youngsters rode toboggans on the snowy mounds. Local businesspeople set up shanties on the ice and sold souvenirs, lunches, tobacco and liquor. A news account in 1888, in describing the activity on the ice bridge, noted, "The several shanties were doing a good business" and visitors to the cataracts on that cold day "must have numbered fully 20,000."

The ice bridge, forty to fifty feet thick, was considered safe for pedestrian traffic and small shanties. But all that changed with striking suddenness on that chill day in 1912. The players were Mr. and Mrs. Eldridge Stanton of Toronto and Burrell Hecock of Cleveland. Mrs. Stanton was twenty-eight; her husband was thirty-six. They had no children after several years of marriage. Stanton was an official in a stationery firm in Toronto. Hecock, seventeen, and his lifelong buddy Ignatius Roth, also seventeen, were on a winter holiday at the same time as the Stantons.

The Stantons and Hecock and Roth were on the ice bridge that fateful Sunday morning browsing among the shanties, taking in the view and strolling on the solid ice formation shortly before noon. At the same time, a huge block of ice lunged over the falls and thudded into the ice bridge, wrenching it loose from its frozen moorings on each shore. If it had happened later in the afternoon, news accounts said, there probably would have been hundreds of tourists on the ice bridge.

Vendors and tourists alike made a mad dash for shore when they heard the thunderous crunching of the ice and felt the movement. The Stantons made for the American shore while Hecock and Roth took off for the Canadian side. Mrs. Stanton fell, and Stanton called for the youths to help him pick up his wife. Hecock, in a single moment of gallantry and heroism went to the aid of the couple. Roth hesitated.

Hecock and the Stantons moved toward the American shore, but by that time the ice was too far from the shore. They turned to try the Canadian side. Roth continued on, and by the time he reached the Canadian side, the ice was quite far from shore. Rescuers threw him a rope and pulled him to safety through the icy water.

The ice broke up further, leaving Hecock on one floe and Mr. and Mrs. Stanton on another. The strong current began moving them downriver toward the treacherous white water of the lower rapids and the whirlpool.

Fire departments of both U.S. and Canadian Niagara Falls rushed to the bridges. Hundreds of spectators gathered as word of mouth quickly spread the news. A group of railroad workers were at the Cantilever Bridge. They obtained a long rope, tied an iron bar to the bottom and dropped it over the side in Hecock's direction. He grabbed the rope, was dunked waist high into the frigid water and then the railroad men began slowly pulling him to the bridge some 190 feet above. Instead of just hanging on, Hecock attempted a hand-over-hand climb up the rope. People began to cheer as he moved closer and closer to safety, but the numbing cold took its toll and his hands began to slip.

Hecock, in a last desperate attempt at life, tried to grasp the rope with his teeth. Then he fell, plummeted thirty feet to an ice floe and stood up momentarily. A wave hit. He was washed over and disappeared into his icy, watery grave. Spectators screamed and wept openly.

Meanwhile, ropes were also thrown to the Stantons, who were some distance behind Hecock. They were unable to grasp the ropes. They watched Hecock's futile rescue attempt and saw him meet his death.

Nearly an hour had passed since the ice bridge first broke up. Under the Lower Arch Bridge, farther down the river, Stanton managed to grab a rope. He tried to tie it around his wife, but the rope broke. Then the ice floe was swamped and they, too, were swept to their deaths.

# Viewing the Falls

Among historians, the puzzle of who was the first white man to view the falls of Niagara is akin to philosophers arguing about how many angels can sit on the head of a pin. You pay your money and make your choices. The early French explorers and fur trappers who traveled the Neuter Indian territory, which included the falls, came as early as 1610. But if any did stumble across the falls, he left no written account.

Franciscan missionary Father Joseph De La Roche Daillon was in the region in 1626, but he did not write about the falls. Jesuit Father Gabriel L'Allemant wrote a letter about the travels of Fathers Jean de Brebeuf and Joseph Marie Chaumonot to the Neuter Nation, but he did not mention whether they viewed the falls. However, a 1928 article by the Old Fort Niagara Association said the two priests visited the Neuter village of Ongiara, the site of present-day Lewiston. If this is the case, it is likely they visited the falls but did not write about it. Ducreaux, in his book *Historiae Canadensis*, noted the falls on a map dated 1660, but he did not mention them in the narrative.

Father Paul Ragueneau in 1648 wrote, "South of the Neuter nation is a great lake called Erie about 200 leagues in circumference, into which is discharged the Fresh Sea, or Lake Huron. This Lake Erie is precipitated by a cataract of frightful height into a third lake called Ontario and by us St. Louis." But he did not say he viewed the falls, nor did he describe them.

Generally attributed with being the first white man to view the falls was Father Louis Hennepin in 1678. He wrote an extensive description of the falls, overestimating their height at six hundred feet. He wrote:

> *The waters which fall from this vast height do foam and boil after the most hideous manner imaginable making an outrageous noise, more terrible than that of thunder.*
>
> *The two brinks of it are so prodigious high that it would make one tremble to look steadily upon the water rolling along with a rapidity not to be imagined. Were it not for this vast cataract, which interrupts navigation, they might sail with barks or greater vessels above the four hundred and fifty leagues further across the lake of Hurons and up to the farther end of the Lake Illinois* [Michigan] *which two lakes we may well say are little seas of fresh water.*

A mural by Thomas Hart Benton depicts Father Hennepin first viewing the falls. The mural is in the Power Vista of the Power Authority of New York. *Photo courtesy of the Power Authority.*

One maritime historian, Donald S. Johnson, trying to discern the truths of history, noted in his book *LaSalle, a Perilous Odyssey from Canada to the Gulf of Mexico* that "sometimes myth and legend form a surer degree of truth and reality than the mere collection of facts." Johnson, a guest curator at the Osher Map Library of the University of Southern Maine and a maritime historian, wrote about Hennepin and LaSalle's trip to the falls area, noting that not all historians have treated LaSalle kindly.

> *Even Father Hennepin, who in his later volume on the history of Louisiana usurped the credit from LaSalle for his discoveries, paid homage to LaSalle for his twenty years of unremitting efforts to bring Christianity to the barbarous savages. To Hennepin, Rene Robert Cavelier de LaSalle was "a man of considerable merit, constant in adversities, fearless, generous, courteous, learned and capable of everything."*

Pierre Francois Xavier de Charlevoix wrote about LaSalle in 1774 in *History of New France*:

> *Such is the lot of those men whom a mixture of great defects and great virtues draws from the common sphere. Their passions hurry them into faults; and if they do what others could not, their enterprises are not to the taste of all men. Their success executes jealousy of those who remain in obscurity. They benefit some and injure others; the latter take their revenge by decrying them without moderation; the former exaggerate their merit.*

*Hence the different portraits drawn of them, none of which are really true, but as hatred and itching for slander always go further than gratitude and friendship and calumny finds more easy credence with the public than praise and eulogy, the enemies of the Sieur de LaSalle disfigured his portrait more than his friends embellished it.*

LaSalle began his career as a Jesuit, but left the order. Hennepin was a Recollect friar. The Recollects and Sulpician Catholic priests, along with Jesuits, were among the first in New France to try to convert natives to Christianity. Sulpician and Recollet friars were of the Franciscan order. The Sulpicians, founded in Paris in 1641, maintained a parish church in Montreal and missions at various sites along the Great Lakes. Recollets were a reformed branch of the order founded by Saint Francis of Assisi early in the thirteenth century. They arrived in New France in 1615 and preceded the Jesuits in establishing missions along the Saint Lawrence River.

René Galinée, a mapmaker who accompanied LaSalle on some expeditions, wrote in his journal that he had heard about the cataracts in an expedition nine years earlier than Hennepin's sighting. Galinée said Indians described to him how, in the river above the falls,

*the current very often sucks into its gulf from a great distance deer and stags, elk and roebucks that suffer themselves to be drawn from such a point in crossing the river that they are compelled to descend the falls and to be overwhelmed in its frightful abyss.*

Galinée said that the thunderous roar from the falls was so great he could hear it from thirty to thirty-six miles away. However, he never gave any indication that he traveled up to the cataracts from Lake Ontario to view the abyss for himself.

Aside from the falls themselves, one of the most significant places is Niagara University, founded in 1856 by Catholic priests of the Congregation of the Missions Order. Father John Lynch and Father John Monaghan, with the aid of Buffalo diocese Bishop John Timon, bought a farm just north of Niagara Falls to start a Catholic seminary. From that humble beginning, Niagara University grew to be an imposing educational force.

The first basketball team was also noted for the school's first basketball star and leading scorer, a young Californian named Gregory Peck, who would later father the distinguished actor and movie star bearing the same name.

Niagara University as it appeared in 1868. *Photo courtesy of Niagara University.*

Niagara University's first basketball team. Star forward Gregory Peck, father of the famed movie actor, is shown first from left in the second row. *Photo courtesy of Niagara University.*

# Clarksville

Histories of Niagara Falls concentrate on the villages of Manchester, Suspension Bridge and LaSalle, but tiny Clarksville is given short shrift, even though it was in the heart of the consolidation area. Perhaps it is often overlooked because Clarksville never made it to the official status of village but remained a hamlet until it was absorbed by Niagara Falls. Nomenclature also changed over the years, adding to the confusion.

Niagara Falls was first called the village of Manchester. Suspension Bridge was called variously Bellevue and Niagara City. But good old Clarksville, located between the two behemoth metropolitan areas, was always known as Clarksville. However, the name faded into history when Suspension Bridge and Niagara Falls merged into a city and LaSalle was later added on.

According to local historian and newspaper editor Orrin E. Dunlap, the boundaries of Clarksville were the Niagara River gorge on the west, the alley between Elmwood and Spruce Avenues on the south, the alley between Nineteenth and Twentieth Streets on the east and the north side of Ashland Avenue on the north. In those days, however, Ashland was Ash Street and Elmwood was Elm Street. Clarksville was thus sandwiched between Suspension Bridge and Niagara Falls.

This hamlet was named after prominent entrepreneur Henry Wells Clark, who came to Niagara Falls from Rochester, where he had been employed in a paper mill. He was born in Pittsfield, Massachusetts, on October 9, 1797, and he learned the papermaking business in Dalton, Massachusetts. He came to Niagara Falls to take advantage of the waterpower and get into the papermaking business. A strange twist of fate, unfortunate for another papermaker named Jesse Symonds, provided Clark with a great opportunity.

Symonds came to Niagara Falls in 1823, a short time before Clark arrived, and began building a paper mill on the mainland near Goat Island. However, Symonds suffered a strange malady for those days and disappeared from his home on June 17, 1823, when he left to visit a doctor. The *Niagara Sentinel* newspaper of Lewiston wrote:

> *Mr. Jesse Symonds, a very respectable and enterprising inhabitant of this village* [Manchester] *had for some days been afflicted with ill health and for some nights had enjoyed little or no sleep.*

*He last evening between the hours of seven and eight left his house for the purpose of calling upon the physician of this place to obtain some composing medicine.*

When he didn't return home, a search was instituted and his hat and coat

*were discovered upon a log which projected into the river a few rods above the pitch of the falls. The presumption is that in a fit of delirium he had thrown himself into the river and in a few seconds ere life could be extinct his body was precipitated down the falls.*

Clark took advantage of this unfortunate circumstance by renting the paper mill started by Symonds, completing the construction and beginning a prosperous business. Three years later, Clark joined with the prominent Porter family in building a new and larger paper mill on Porter property located on Bath Island, later called Green Island, near Goat Island.

This first papermaking situation led to an error in print, and perhaps the most intriguing correction I have ever noted in many years in the news business. A rhyming historian named Barlow, whose works were discovered by Dunlap, wrote two volumes of *Village Days in Old Niagara Falls*. In his first volume, he said the Symonds paper mill was started in 1826. His second volume contained this correction:

*And so permit me to explain,*
*I've promised to and will,*
*And my mistake was all anent*
*Our first built paper mill.*

*I place the date—'twas long before*
*My memory could fix,*
*So placed the date—as I was told,*
*At Eighteen Twenty-six;*
*Twas in the spring of '23*
*That Jesse Symonds came,*
*Leased site for mill, at once began*
*Erection of the same.*

*Death came to him in early fall,*
*Ere yet the mill was done,*

*The widow's brother finished what*
*The husband had begun,*
*A three years lease was given then*
*To Henry W. Clark,*
*And paper made here bore for years*
*His well-known watermark.*

*So I was wrong about the date*
*Of papermaking here,*
*Bout who was first in building line,*
*As well as of the year;*
*To give the proper credit here*
*The chance I gladly take,*
*That Symond's was the first to build*
*And Clark the first to make.*

Somehow, it seems to me, the poetic aspect takes the embarrassing sting out of admitting one made a mistake in print.

Clark did well in his papermaking venture and bought up much land in the center of the city, where he had his home on the northeast corner of Main and Elmwood. Everyone began calling this little hamlet Clarksville.

Clark was elected supervisor of the Town of Niagara, which included the whole area at that time, and he served from 1827 to 1830 and was elected again in 1836, 1838 and 1861. He also served as president of the Village of Niagara Falls in the 1860s and then became prominent in the railroad business.

Clark was held in high regard as a railroad agent, a position he held for forty years. The *Niagara City Herald* at Suspension Bridge, noting a new railroad engine that bore Clark's name, wrote on May 8, 1856:

*Mr. Clark has been receiver and superintendent of the depot of the place nearly a quarter of a century and no individual has ever discharged his duties more assiduously and impartially than that gentleman. We feel proud that the company has paid him a compliment so justly his due.*

A few days later, on May 14, 1856, the *Niagara Falls Times* wrote:

*Our neighbor at the Bridge pays our townsman H.W. Clark, a well deserved compliment in saying that as receiver and local superintendent of the N.Y.C.R.R. at this place ".No individual ever discharged his duties more assiduously and impartially." He has occupied this position for a long time, a fact of itself complimentary in the highest degree. An engine bearing his name has lately been put on the road.*

Residents of the tiny hamlet of Clarksville decided to end their isolated existence and join the growing community around the falls. In the latter part of the 1880s, there was a growing trend to merge the settlements around the falls even though much of that area was still forested or cleared farmland. Residents of Clarksville did not want to be left out.

On February 26, 1887, a petition signed by thirty-nine prominent residents of Clarksville was presented to State Assemblyman Peter A. Porter seeking union with Niagara Falls. The first name on the petition was that of J.F. Trott, a son-in-law of Cataract House and Eagle Tavern owner Parkhurst Whitney.

The petition stated:

*We the undersigned, inhabitants of the hamlet called Clarksville and all the land lying between the north line of Clarksville and the south line of the Village of Suspension Bridge, and bounded on the east by Portage Road and on the west by the Niagara River, the said territory hereby designated being and lying in the Town of Niagara, State of New York, do hereby respectfully petition your honorable body that the above territory and inhabitants may be incorporated with and made part of the Village of Niagara Falls, State of New York, Town of Niagara.*

The state legislature passed the bill on April 19, 1887, and Clarksville became a part of the village of Niagara Falls. Charles B. Gaskill was president of the village when the application was begun, but Hiram E. Griffith was president when the measure became law.

A few years later, residents of Suspension Bridge, just north of Clarksville, did not want to be left out and so petitioned to become a part of the expanding community to the south. The merger was completed, and on March 17, 1892, the village of Niagara Falls, hamlet of Clarksville and village of Suspension Bridge became the city of Niagara Falls.

While petty jealousies between the communities had existed in the past, it seems there was nothing but harmony at the time of the mergers. Historian Dunlap noted the *Niagara Falls Gazette* "made no editorial comment, simply announcing passage of the bill."

When the application was begun, the Gaskill administration was Republican, and by the time the merger passed, the Democratic administration of President Griffith had taken over. But neither Republicans nor Democrats had any objections to the merger.

Part of Parkhurst Whitney's farm was in Clarksville and that is why his son-in-law, J.F. Trott, signed the petition-seeking merger. Whitney retired to that farm, leaving operation of the Cataract House to his son-in-law. In writing about retirement in 1846, Whitney said:

> *During the above period* [when he was running the hotel] *I changed my circumstances from making my own fire, being hostler, tending bar, waiting on tables, my wife doing the cooking, all together, four or five servants, to the employment of one hundred servants and giving up the establishment to the children and returning to my old calling of farming.*

Regarding Clark's papermaking skills, a traveling writer, one Joseph Wentworth Ingraham of Boston, Massachusetts, included a tract about Clark in his book about Niagara Falls. He wrote, "The paper mill of Messrs. Porter and Clark is on this Island [Bath, later Green Island]." He described the building and its equipment and then noted, "I have myself tried their letter and writing paper and pronounce it good. Of their printing paper the reader may judge for himself as this tract is a specimen of it, though they may sometimes manufacture that which is of much better quality." He added:

> *I would have this little tract printed on better paper if it could have been procured in this vicinity, but it may add some interest to the book in the eyes of visitors to be informed that the paper on which it is printed was manufactured at the Falls and the waters of Niagara, therefore, are intimately blended with its every fibre. It may be added, too, that the printing has been executed within view of the spray arising from the falls. That also may be some recommendation.*

The book was dated July 1, 1834.

The Clark homestead was on property deeded to Augustus Porter by the Holland Land Company in 1814 and by Porter to Asa Pierce in 1829. Pierce built the house and sold it to Clark in 1836. Clark later took residence on First Street and deeded the homestead to his son, Thomas E. Clark, who never occupied the house but rented it to a tenant farmer. A fire destroyed the house on August 25, 1883, ostensibly set by youngsters playing around a bonfire. A couple of large haystacks nearby added to the intensity of the blaze.

In the earlier days of the hamlet, there was a low spot in the street just north of Elmwood Avenue. In wet periods a small creek ran through there down to the gorge. So that carriages could pass, a corduroy road (logs placed side by side) was built in that section. An 1827 map shows that the name of the road from Main Street in the village of Niagara Falls, through Clarksville to Suspension Bridge was named Road to Lewiston. Later, Niagara Falls named its section Ontario Street and Suspension Bridge called it Lewiston Avenue. When the villages merged, it became Main Street.

In the earlier days, there was a planked sidewalk through a portion of Clarksville. The planks, in an economic move, were not laid side by side but were separated by turf. This sidewalk was the subject of a letter to the editor by one Miss Walker on February 23, 1859. She wrote:

> *Mr. Editor, As the subject of annexation again seems to be rife both in private and public life, it has occurred to me that while discussing the merits of annexing Cuba and Canada, we might advantageously confine our efforts nearer home and by a trifling exertion do an act of real benefit and convenience to a large class of our citizens.*

She wanted the plank sidewalk extended; she said that the unplanked distance was about two thousand feet and residents along that section favored such action. She wrote, "By carrying out the excellent plan already begun, of laying plank with sod between, the expense of the interval will be trifling." She exhorted the editor to "bring your formidable influence to bear on the public spirit in your readers and adopt some prompt and practicable plan to effect this desirable object."

Henry W. Clark died at his First Street residence on November 11, 1873.

# Cave of the Winds

A rather humorous controversy erupted in 1834 about the first person to enter the famed and long-hidden Cave of the Winds. One Joseph Ingraham, of Boston, indicated in a Niagara Falls guidebook he wrote that the honor belonged to him. Another contemporary guidebook writer, Horatio A. Parsons, wrote that the credit should belong to him, but he conceded that he "pooped out" and two of his companions were actually the first to enter the cave.

Late city historian Donald Loker seemed to favor giving the credit to Ingraham, while Falls newspaper editor and historian Orrin E. Dunlap favored Parsons's story. Dunlap, in fact, wrote a treatise on the subject to present a clearer picture of the occurrences.

Parsons wrote a Falls guidebook in 1829, and Ingraham had his guidebook printed in 1834, the year the cave was entered. In fact, Ingraham indicated his discovery was so new that he could only publicize it in an addendum pasted in the back of his guidebook that had already been printed. The addendum, dated July 15, 1834, proclaimed, "I have found it," and later added, "Reader! Do you not congratulate me!" However, according to Dunlap, Parsons wrote credibly that the cave had been entered on July 15, 1834, by two of Parsons's companions.

Dunlap wrote that there had been speculation about such a cave for years, but

> it was not until ferry boats were operated on the lower river and the Biddle stairway had been erected on the gorge face of Goat Island that venturesome white men sought to be first to go behind the sheet of falling water. Their desire to pierce the mystery actually grew into rivalry between several of the men who hovered about the falls awaiting the day when the elements involved would permit them to attain the honor of first entering the suspected cavern.

Dunlap wrote, "In 1833 there came to Niagara Falls a man named Joseph Wentworth Ingraham, of Boson, Massachusetts." And he became enthralled with the falls and the cave. "He had been to Niagara twice before July 1, 1834, and on each visit gathered information for his contemplated writings."

A Cave of the Winds engraving by Amos W. Sanger, 1886.

Ingraham claimed that, upon his urging, Judge Augustus Porter, owner of Goat Island, agreed to improve access to the cave by having "a timber carried out and a ladder attached to it so that visitors who are daring may descend and explore the secrets of this Cave of the Winds."

However, Parsons wrote that, since the Biddle staircase was erected in 1829, thousands of people approached the cave to view its wonders. "The name very properly given it at first, and the name by which it has ever been known, is Aeolus Cave, or Cave of the Winds. Aeolus was the fabled God of the winds." Parsons graciously admitted that the path to the cave was improved by Judge Porter upon the urging of Ingraham and "for this request, Mr. Ingraham is entitled to all the credit it deserves."

He went on to write that even though Ingraham claimed "he originated the idea and pointed out the practicability of entering" the cave, "why did he not first enter it and obtain the glory he so much desired?" Parsons added,

The present-day Cave of the Winds walk taking tourists up to the cave site.

"The fact was that his idea of originating the plan, etc., was never heard of till after the cave had been entered by others."

Parsons said he first conceived the idea of "entering it by passing around outside of the center fall and of descending from the foot of Luna Island." With a rope tied around him and held by companions, he almost made it to the cave on July 15, 1834. He wrote that, in desperation after several failures, he "made a bold plunge with a rope tied around" him in order "to cross the stream that rushed down between the rocks and, after much struggling was finally drawn back under the foam in a state of almost perfectly bodily exhaustion."

While he was resting, two of his companions, "G.H. White and George W. Sims, succeeded in crossing the stream and entering the cave from the foot of Luna Island. To them belonged all the glory of first entering it, but the practicability of thus entering it and the cause of its being then explored are fairly attributed to this writer [Parsons]." He then wrote, "On a subsequent day, the cave was entered the same way by another party and on another day by a third party, of whom Mr. Ingraham was one."

According to Dunlap, three witnesses to the feat signed an affidavit as follows:

> *We the subscribers hereby certify that we were present when G.H. White and George W. Sims entered this day The Cavern of the Winds; that they penetrated what appeared to us to be the extreme end of said cavern, we having been so situated as to command at intervals of a good view of the same, and we have been candidly informed and believe that they are the first and only persons who have ever entered the said cavern.*

It was signed by James B. Henshaw, New York; D. Lydig Syndam, New York; and George B. Shaw, Virginia.

From that date until 1920, Dunlap wrote, the cave was a leading attraction. But in 1920, rock falls caused the state reservation officials to stop "entrance to the cave, since which time visitors have enjoyed the trip about the bridges in front of the famous cave to the Hurricane Deck, so called."

# PART V

# *Historical Flotsam*

# Simms's Cow

The recent rescue of a man standing near the brink of the Horseshoe Falls was an astounding feat, but a nineteenth-century cow accomplished the same feat, repeatedly, at the brink of the more deadly American Falls. As improbable as this seems, it comes from no less an authority than Peter A. Porter, historian, businessman and publisher. It is contained in his *Niagara Falls Guide Book* published in 1901.

Tourist guidebooks can sometimes exaggerate to catch the visitors' attention, telling such apocryphal stories as a cat in the barrel with Annie Edson Taylor when she was the first person to go over the falls in a barrel. But sage county historian, the late Clarence O. Lewis, wrote that he believed the cow story. In 1954 he stated, "The Porter family has lived in Niagara Falls since 1806 and anything that emanates from them is pretty certain to be authentic so we may accept this story as true."

Porter, who was also instrumental in forming the Pioneer Association of Niagara County and in contributing to the association's history book of the county, said in his guidebook that the incidents occurred in 1860. A man named Simms was superintendent of the inclined railcars that took tourists to the base of the falls at Prospect Point.

Niagara Falls was sparsely settled at that time, Porter wrote, so Simms lived nearby on land large enough to graze a cow. This brave, or foolhardy, bovine took to wading out into the swift current near the brink of the American Falls, much to the astonishment of both Simms and tourists. She did this not once, but made a routine of it so that the residents gave her the name Bossy Simms. Once, Bossy Simms made it all the way across to Goat Island. As a sort of impromptu tourist attraction, the cow would often turn her enigmatic gaze at curious tourists while chewing her cud in the rushing waters.

Simms seemed to have no fear of losing his milk producer and was amused over the antics of his cow. It undoubtedly drew more spectators to Prospect

A picture of the American Falls in 1894 for sale to tourists.

Point as potential customers for his rail incline to the bottom. But there was a fly in the ointment. Other tourist operators and hackmen, perhaps over competitive jealousy, became upset. They claimed the cow's defiance of the mighty and terrifying cataract with apparent ease made a mockery of the power, majesty and inherent danger of the falls. They demanded that the cow be restrained from its river walks.

The clamor became so much that Simms finally agreed to keep his cow confined to the pasture and away from the brink of the falls. However, not to be outdone by a mere animal, local river man Joel Robinson in 1860 decided to duplicate the feat. It may be remembered that Robinson was the captain who took the *Maid of the Mist* downriver, through the horrific whirlpool to Lewiston when it was sold. That occurred in 1861.

Porter's guidebook also tells of Robinson's walking feat. Robinson fashioned a sharpened steel pole to use as a support, waded out into the dangerous water and made it across to Goat Island. He may have gotten his idea from reports of earlier Native Americans who used such staffs to wade to Goat Island before bridges were built. However, the Indians waded to the island near the eastern end, farther away from the brink of the American Falls.

It is not often that I get a column handed to me, but this addendum to the saga of Bossy, the death-defying cow who waded near the brink of the falls, and Captain Robinson, who did the same, is too good to pass up. I have heard from doubters out there who have witnessed the ferocious power of water pounding over the falls and could not believe a cow or a person could walk through it. I must confess that I had my doubts. But then I heard from a couple of different descendants of Mr. Simms and Captain Robinson, Anne Brophy and Susan Martin, both of Niagara Falls.

I received an email from a descendant of the cow's owner, John Simms, who wanted to correct me on the spelling of the last name. In the spirit of journalistic objectivity, I pass on to you this rather mild criticism and the added information provided by Anne Brophy:

*Dear Mr. Kostoff,*

*I always enjoy reading your local history column. I have been a student of our local stories for most of my life.*

*I was very interested to see the story about the cow at the brink of the falls. The Sims (only one "m") were my paternal grandmother's family. They were in this area at least as early as 1805. At that time John Sims was working for the Porters, bringing supplies over the Portage between Fort Niagara and the upper river. The family moved into the present park area and were there until the state took over the land. They worked for the Porter family for most of that time.*

*When the grandchildren ask me if any of our ancestors are famous I always explain about our cow. Bossy is the favorite story that they take to school when they are studying local history or doing a show and tell. I have a picture of Bossy standing at the brink of the falls. I always understood the tourists would annoy her with patting her and trying to feed her until she would walk out into the water to get away from them.*

*My great-grandfather, George Sims, ran the incline railway, as you mentioned. This trip to the base of the falls has been a tourist attraction since George began running the railway. When the tourists asked him about the danger of the railway breaking and falling down the gorge, he would tell them not to worry. "We collect the money before you start the ride." In his obituary, it mentions that he was a great favorite with the tourists as he had lived in the park all his life and knew many stories and local lore to share with them.*

*Before the bridges were built, first brothers John and then George used to row visitors back and forth across the river. It's possible John rowed people across the river above the falls before the settlement moved down into the present park. I also have a ferry ticket for this pre–*Maid of the Mist *tourist attraction.*

*George was also known for being one of the two boys who first discovered the Cave of the Winds behind the American Falls. One day the friends were sitting at the edge of the cliff on Goat Island and they noticed the birds flying into the falling water and not coming back out. They decided to climb down and see where the birds were going and made their way behind the falls and into the cave. Again they were the start of a major tourist attraction.*

*Thank you for your story, adding a little more shine to our famous family cow!*
*Anne Brophy*

And here is an excerpt of the email from Susan Martin, the descendant of Captain Joel Robinson:

*Hi Bob, I enjoyed your article in the* Niagara Falls Reporter *April 6–13 2004, titled "bovine braved the rapids" especially the tidbit about Joel Robinson who was my great, great, great, grandfather. I don't know much about him other than he did pilot the* Maid of the Mist *through the whirlpool rapids to Queenston and on to Lake Ontario.*

*I did not know that he fashioned a steel pole to use as a support and waded out to Goat Island. He must have liked water to do both those crazy stunts. It is a shame that Joel is not mentioned more as the local kids nowadays have no idea who he was.*
*Susan Martin.*

Thanks Anne and Susan.

# The Griffon

The fate of *The Griffon*, explorer LaSalle's historic ship lost somewhere in the Great Lakes, has intrigued historic detectives for hundreds of years. A Canadian journalist claims to have solved the mystery. John MacLean, in his 1974 book *The Fate of* The Griffon, is convinced the remains of an old ship found in a remote cove off Georgian Bay, not far from Tobermory, Ontario, are those of LaSalle's ship. And he has convinced some Canadian experts.

MacLean's involvement came in 1955 when he was a reporter for the *Toronto Telegram*. An acquaintance living at Tobermory, Orrie Vail, told him of finding old wreckage in the cove. MacLean got permission from his editor to pursue the story.

Vail said his grandfather and father knew of the wreckage. He himself said, "I've gone over to look at her hundreds of times." He even salvaged some parts of the stern and brought up old nails and bolts. The remaining wreckage, he said, included "the entire keel, bow, stern, thirteen ribs and quite a bit of planking on the port side."

MacLean's research ruled out other reported discoveries of *The Griffon*. The first one was the discovery of an anchor and two cannons in Lake Erie near Hamburg, another at Fitzwilliam Island in Georgian Bay and another at Manitoulin Island in that area. All proved to be ships other than *The Griffon*.

One sticking point was that the length of the keel in the Vail find indicated the ship was about forty tons burthen. Father Louis Hennepin, who accompanied LaSalle in his explorations, in one book said *The Griffon* was forty-two tons and in a later writing that it was sixty "tuns." MacLean learned that, in historic mariner terms, "tons" was dead weight while "tuns" was "not a weight but the cubic space a barrel occupies in stowage." Thus, a ship of forty tons burthen could carry sixty tuns of cargo.

Some historians have questioned Hennepin's accuracy in writing about LaSalle's explorations in the New World. In his second book, published in 1697 after LaSalle had died, Hennepin took most of the credit for the explorations. He wrote, "I am resolved to make known here to the whole world the mystery of this discovery which I have hitherto concealed that I might not offend Sieur de LaSalle, who wished to keep all the glory and the knowledge of it to himself."

MacLean came across a letter in archives stored in Montreal written by LaSalle to LaMotte. LaSalle was at the shipbuilding site in the Little River

An engraving of the building of LaSalle's ship *The Griffon* in Niagara Falls as found in Father Hennepin's 1697 book about explorations in America.

near the mouth of Cayuga Creek, and LaMotte was at the Lewiston Landing where provisions were stored. LaSalle requested that more goods be brought to the shipbuilding site, including food and ammunition. For himself, LaSalle requested, "I will also need three pairs of snowshoes, my hat, my wig, a dressed and oiled skin as well as a bearskin, soap and three jars of wine or thereabouts." He also ordered that those bringing up the goods hunt wild game for their food on the way. To make sure, he had LaMotte "record the weight thereof for Lucas to verify at this end." The construction site was where Cayuga Creek in the LaSalle section of Niagara Falls flows into the Niagara River a few miles above the falls. The site today is marked by a historic plaque on a boulder.

One of the bolts Vail found was without threads but held by a washer and a wedge into a slit in the bottom of the bolt. MacLean learned from marine experts that threaded bolts did not come into use in shipbuilding until after *The Griffon* was built. He also had a sliver of the salvaged wood analyzed and it turned out to be white oak, which Hennepin indicated was used to construct *The Griffon*. Vail and MacLean brought up the rest of the wreckage and stored it at Vail's place at Tobermory for inspection by experts.

MacLean brought in two experts to examine remains of the wreckage. The experts were Rowley W. Murphy, a marine architect and artist, and C.H.J. Snider, a world-recognized authority on early shipping and a member of Britain's exclusive Society for Nautical Research. MacLean and Vail took them in an outboard to the isolated cove off Russell Island in Georgian Bay where the wreck lay underwater for centuries. Then they returned to Vail's work shed, where the salvaged parts of the wreckage were stored. They wrote a lengthy report that ended with, "We have decided that the Tobermory wreck found in Russell Island fills all the information we have as to the size and shape of *The Griffon*. We can accept the Tobermory recovery as *The Griffon*."

MacLean and Vail were overjoyed. But MacLean was nagged by a lingering mystery. He wrote, "It's just that I'm concerned about the location. If *The Griffon* was headed for Niagara Falls after leaving LaSalle in Green Bay, how could she end up here?" For the answer, he turned to Hennepin's writings about the ship's maiden voyage through the Great Lakes to Mackinac, where LaSalle learned some in his advance party had deserted to Sault Saint Marie. He sent his second in command, Iron Hand Tonti, thirty miles north to apprehend the deserters. The ship moved on to Green Bay to pick up the furs.

LaSalle was waiting for Tonti's return so Tonti could command the ship back to Niagara while LaSalle moved down the Illinois River, continuing his explorations. However, Tonti was delayed. The bad winter weather was approaching, so LaSalle sent a small crew under command of his pilot, a Dane named Lucas.

Hennepin wrote, "LaSalle, without asking any body's advice resolved to send back his ship to Niagara laden with furs and skins to discharge his debts. Our pilot and five men with him were therefore sent back." They left on September 18, 1680.

When the group left, that was the last LaSalle saw or heard of his boat or the pilot and crew. He later received word that a pack of moldy beaver skins had been cast up on Mackinac Island. Rumors spread that the ship foundered in a storm or was attacked and burned by Indians. There were even suspicions that Lucas and the crew scuttled the ship to make off with the rich furs.

MacLean wrote about his personal belief after much research. *The Griffon* "didn't drift into her grave. It wasn't happenchance that robbed the explorer of his ship." To get to the wreckage location, *The Griffon* "was carefully steered into the narrow channel entrance to the first cove. Then she was turned to a bearing of 240 degrees. Then she was angled four degrees to the starboard and probably towed through the next and narrower channel by men on shore." At that stage in history, he said, the only people who would know of such a secluded cove were Native Americans. But, he said, they would not have had the expertise to maneuver such a ship into that location.

MacLean believes the pilot Lucas and the crew wanted to steal the furs so they picked up some Indians, and the Indians directed them into Georgian Bay and the isolated cove. Then the ship was scuttled and the crew made off with the furs. Or, perhaps the Indians turned the tables, killed the crew, sunk the ship and stole the furs.

A French historian, La Poutherie, who published a book in 1753, wrote that the pilot Lucas, at a stop on the return trip, met some Indians "and received them with entire good will, but the opportunity seemed to them at the moment too advantageous to miss their stroke." He said they "slew all the Frenchmen, carried away all the goods that suited them and burned the barque." LaSalle, he wrote, after showing Indians "tokens of esteem and friendship…had never suspected such perfidy and believed his ship had been wrecked."

The mysteries of history, like time, march on inexorably. Such is the case of LaSalle's lost ship *The Griffon*. But then, along comes another claim. And this claim was tied up in federal court action and even international intrigue.

Fellow LaSalle High School graduate, the late David A. Bright, who was president of Nautical Research Group, Inc., brought this to my attention. He was involved in underwater and shipwreck exploration for almost thirty-five years and, in fact, he lost his life in a dive at the sunken *Andrea Doria*. A research scientist with a scientific degree in biology and an advanced degree in physiology from the Pennsylvania State University, he was an experienced shipwreck historian and deep technical diver. He worked in various capacities on more than thirty-five documentaries with such networks as National Geographic, the Discovery Channel, the History Channel, A&E, the Learning Channel and PBS (Public Broadcasting).

A Great Lakes treasure hunter, Steve Libert, claimed he found the wreck of *The Griffon* between Escanaba and the Saint Martin islands off Michigan. However, the state of Michigan claimed the wreck, saying state law and the federal Abandoned Shipwreck Act gave the state ownership of sunken boats of historical significance. Michigan filed suit against Libert and his Great

Lakes Exploration Group, blocking any work at the site. Libert's lawyer claimed Libert "was committed to preserving the site" and wanted to work with Michigan officials.

However, instead of negotiating with the state, Libert performed a reverse-end run with an international angle and negotiated with the French government. Thus, France staked a claim to the wreck, noting *The Griffon* had been commissioned as a French vessel on officially sanctioned French business. Explorer LaSalle, accompanied by Father Louis Hennepin, had been in the process of exploring the Great Lakes and Mississippi regions for the French king when *The Griffon* was built at the mouth of Cayuga Creek where it empties into the Niagara River.

France decided to exert its international right to the wreckage and appointed Libert and his group to continue their salvage work on behalf of the French government. The question then arose as to who had jurisdiction. Did international law supersede State of Michigan law?

Bright said at the time, "The story of *The Griffon* is still shrouded by mystery and now international litigation." Bright succumbed after scuba diving July 8, 2006, off Nantucket Island, Massachusetts.

# *Cold Case* Mystery

An unsolved murder mystery involving the falls of Niagara in the nineteenth century seems worthy of a modern-day *Cold Case* episode. It involved a troubled Niagara Falls resident, his seemingly sympathetic brother-in-law and a grisly crime on Goat Island. But exactly what transpired on the dark, cold night near the Bridal Veil Falls remains shrouded in mystery to this day.

The crime occurred on April 9, 1884, with spring rapidly approaching, but cold Niagara Falls weather still lingered, keeping snow and ice on the ground. Van Rensselaer Pearson was an increasingly disturbed family man, who quit his job as a cashier in the New York Central Railroad Office on Falls Street and turned to drink. He became abusive to his wife and children, and seemed to be sinking into insanity. He left a note for his wife on how to dispose of his property if anything should happen to him. He got out a long-unused pistol, cleaned it and restored it to good working order.

A boulder and plaque mark the spot at Cayuga Creek and the Niagara River where *The Griffon* was built.

Pearson's brother-in-law, Thomas Vedder, was worried about his sister Sarah Jane and her family, and he offered his help. The family thought Pearson should seek treatment in a mental institution in Saint Catharines, but how would they convince him to go there?

On that fateful April 9, Vedder decided to take Pearson on a buggy ride and try to talk him into seeking treatment. They left the house late in the afternoon and crossed the toll bridge to Goat Island before 5:30 p.m. When they failed to return home that night, Vedder's brother James and Pearson's son Howard began a search that eventually led them to the Goat Island Bridge. The attendant remembered seeing the two men drive to the island, but had not seen them return. They sought the aid of police.

With the help of kerosene lanterns, they proceeded to Luna Island, where the horse and buggy were parked. They then went down the stone steps to Luna Island and discovered Pearson's body, his head in a pool of blood. Vedder was nowhere to be found, but much of his clothing was neatly folded and piled near the brink of the falls.

While forensic science was not nearly as advanced in those days, an autopsy did reveal that Pearson had been shot twice. One bullet had hit him in the right side of the neck and exited on the left of the chin. The hair was not singed, so the doctor estimated that the shot had been fired from six to twenty-four inches away. A second shot had entered below the left eye and snapped the brain stem, killing Pearson instantly. Powder burns indicated the second shot had been fired from close range.

No gun was found.

A coroner's inquest was convened on April 11. Pearson's other son, Martin, said he believed his father, in a fit of insanity, killed Vedder, either by shooting or strangling him, removed his clothes, tossed him over the brink and neatly piled the clothes. He then shot himself twice with the pistol, which then fell and skittered over ice into the river.

A couple of months later, on June 5, 1884, Vedder's body was found at the base of the Bridal Veil Falls when workers were rebuilding the Cave of the Winds decking. An autopsy disclosed no visible gunshot wounds.

Vedder had been a wealthy merchant who owned a grocery store and much property in the area, including the United States Hotel in Suspension Bridge. He left half of his estate to his sister and her children and his will even provided a token $1,000 to Pearson.

Another theory advanced at the time was that Vedder and Pearson quarreled about the mental treatment, Vedder managed to wrest the gun from Pearson, killed him, then, in a fit of fear and remorse, disrobed, piled his clothes neatly and jumped over the falls.

Still another theory was that some mysterious third party was involved, perhaps one of the heirs who knew of the provisions in Vedder's will. In any event, the mystery was never solved and some inspired reporter of the day wrote, "What transpired between these two, which resulted so fatally, will in all probability remain a secret between them and their Maker."

# Dry Falls

The spectacle of a dry Niagara Falls near the end of the severe winter of 1847–48 was witnessed by many people, but was met with skepticism in later years. Orrin E. Dunlap, local newspaper editor and historian of the 1900s, wrote an interesting essay on the rare occurrence. He told of a Right Reverend Bishop Fuller who lectured on the phenomenon some thirty-two years after it happened.

A local newspaper, whose editor said he thought the story sounded "fishy," picked up on some of the bishop's comments. There were many other skeptics then, and even today the occasional email is received inquiring if the story of the falls running dry was true.

Dunlap wrote, "It is not remarkable that from time to time the river has nearly ceased to flow and the spectacle of a dry Niagara Falls has been created without the interference of any Volstead act." (Dunlap was referring to the 1919 Volstead Act, which initiated Prohibition and turned the whole nation "dry" by outlawing alcoholic beverages.) He continued:

> The first recorded instance of the falls of Niagara going practically dry because of ice and wind conditions was on March 29, 1848 when a truly remarkable phenomenon was witnessed by the then residents and others who hurried to look upon the spectacle of the rocks left bare.

There were no cameras at that time to record the event, but it was carried in Buffalo newspapers and some written declarations of witnesses exist. Dunlap said the severe winter caused a thick ice cap on the shallow Lake Erie. When a spring thaw came at the end of March the ice cap broke loose and, during the day, a strong east wind drove the ice up farther into Lake Erie. "About sundown," he wrote, "the wind shifted and blew a gale from the west. This turned the ice in its course and bringing it back to the entrance of the Niagara River where it piled up in a solid mass."

The natural ice dam reduced the flow of water out of Lake Erie into the Niagara River down to a veritable trickle. "The roaring, tumbling rapids above the falls were almost obliterated," he wrote, adding the rather flowery comment, "the loud roaring of the water's mad leap had subsided into a melancholy moan and the scene was one of desolation."

Dunlap came across a letter that the late Reverend Fuller had written to the *Chicago Tribune* from his home in Hamilton, Ontario. He told of giving a lecture in Hamilton that mentioned the dry falls that had occurred thirty-two years previously. Fuller wrote, "I did not witness it myself, but I was told of it the next day by my brother-in-law, Thomas C. Street, Esq. M.P." His brother-in-law lived at the edge of the falls on the Canadian side and operated a gristmill there.

Street said his miller awakened him at 5:00 a.m. to tell him there was no rushing water in the raceway off the falls to power the gristmill. Fuller said Street "hurried out as soon as he could dress himself and saw the river, on the edge of which he had been born 34 years before, dry." He said that Street and his young daughter, after breakfast, walked to the brink of the falls. Street took a strong pole and together they "started from the Table Rock and walked near the edge of the precipice about one-third of the way toward Goat Island on the American shore, and having stuck his pole in a crevice of the rock and Miss Street having tied her pocket handkerchief firmly on top of the pole, they returned." Street said that, looking down into the gorge, he saw "immense jagged rocks" that "stood up in such a frightful manner that he shuddered when he thought of his having frequently passed over them in the little steamer *Maid of the Mist*."

Fuller said that before delivering the lecture, he had sought confirmation from L.F. Allen, of Buffalo, who wrote back on March 2, 1880, that he had heard of the event and also knew Street well "and should have entire credence in any statement he should make of his own knowledge." Fuller said after the lecture notices appeared in local papers, clips of the story were sent to him along with a comment from an editor who wrote that "some rumors had been afloat at times regarding the matter" but he looked upon it "as rather a fishy story." Fuller also had two written and sworn declarations of the occurrence by witnesses Henry Bond and James Francis Macklem, both of Chippewa.

Dunlap wrote:

> *People were able to walk far out to the brink of the precipice and a horse and buggy were driven far outside the Sisters Islands. The dry rocks were a great distance beyond the old Terrapin Tower at the Horseshoe Falls and huge timbers were drawn from outside the Sister Islands. The river bed remained dry all day, but the next morning it was fairly well restored to a normal condition.*

# Suspension Bridge

The Spanish Aero Car across the Canadian whirlpool in the lower Niagara River has attracted tourists and locals alike for many years. But that conveyance was preceded by a cable car across the lower gorge from the United States to Canada as preliminary work for construction of the first suspension bridge. One of the main architects of the cable car was Judge Theodore G. Hulett, a pioneer of Niagara Falls who was an engineer and who also served thirty years as a justice of the peace.

According to Niagara historian Edward T. Williams in a newspaper article on February 19, 1938, "Judge Hulett made the basket in which passengers first crossed the Niagara gorge on a cable and this basket is now in the possession of the Buffalo Historical Society by written direction of Judge Hulett."

Hulett, born in Williamsburg, Massachusetts, on June 13, 1811, ran away from home at age twelve, became a blacksmith, made his way to Buffalo and then to Niagara Falls where, through self education, he became a civil engineer, bridge builder and jurist.

In writing his reminiscences of Niagara Falls, Judge Hulett detailed the story of how the basket and the first suspension bridge came into being. The story is not without some heroics and daring rescues.

Theodore Hulett, a Niagara Falls engineer, helped build the first suspension bridge to Canada.

Judge Hulett wrote that Charles Ellet Jr., of Philadelphia, an engineer with experience in suspension bridge building, was hired to construct the bridge here. He made a trip to Niagara Falls in the winter of 1847 and summoned Judge Hulett to a meeting at the Eagle Tavern to solicit the judge's help. Ellet said he had another bridge building job in Wheeling and needed someone to take charge of the ironwork in Niagara Falls. Judge Hulett agreed to partner with Ellet in the bridge building venture.

It was at this first meeting that the idea of a preliminary cable car crossing of the gorge was broached. Judge Hulett wrote:

> *The engineer stated in detail his plan of construction. First to provide some means of crossing the gorge with men and tools without crossing at a ferry in Lewiston five miles below, thus saving 10 miles travel for each desired crossing.*

The first suspension bridge over the lower Niagara River gorge linked the United States and Canada in 1847.

Next, the engineers discussed making a basket to hold two men and tools. Ellet suggested making it of wood but Judge Hulett, a much-experienced blacksmith, said it could be made of iron, which was stronger and lighter than wood.

They each drafted plans and, figuring on the weight of materials, discovered Judge Hulett's iron basket was ten pounds lighter than the wooden one. Next, Ellet wondered how it could be built, but Judge Hulett jumped right in, saying, "I assured the engineer that getting it made would present no difficulty as I would make it with my own hands."

Judge Hulett also presented a detailed and highly technical explanation of making a cable sufficient to bear the cable car weight. "This cable," he wrote,

*was to be constructed of 36 strands of number 10 wire, each*
*strand to be subjected to a uniform strain and the 36 strands*

*bound into a round form by being wrapped by a transverse*
*wrapping of a small annealed wire at intervals of eight inches,*
*each wrapping being about four inches in length.*

The engineers then had to decide how to make the initial gorge crossing. They came up with the idea of the now well-told story of having a kite-flying contest across the gorge by offering a ten-dollar prize. The winner, young Homan Walsh of Lockport, received his prize "as soon as the kite string was secured on the bank of the stream." The kite string, of course, was used to draw across a stronger rope, which in turn was used to draw across the cable that was secured to the rock banks. The cable car was hung on the cable on rollers and drawn back and forth by a windlass on each bank.

Hulett wrote, "The first passage of this basket was attempted to be made empty, but when almost across it suddenly stopped and the windlass on the opposite side would not bring it ashore." It could be drawn back, but would not cross to Canada.

Ellet decided to be the first passenger and try to solve this problem. He got in the basket and was drawn to the site of the obstruction, which turned out to be "a spot in the cable that had been flattened when the cable was being hauled across." He fixed the problem easily.

However, they made new rollers with a wider groove. "This change made," Judge Hulett wrote,

*this mode of transportation was complete and it was used for*
*that purpose for more than one year and carried across the gorge*
*more then 2,000 passengers. This cable was used until the*
*preliminary bridge structure was completed and then removed.*

While the bridge was being built, another crisis occurred when a terrific windstorm arose while workers were on the bridge. The unfinished part of the bridge was swinging in the wind for a hundred feet and was finally thrown over the cable car wire. Judge Hulett said there were two workers on the Canadian end who made it safely to land, but there were four workers closer to the American side, with only one making it safely back. He wrote, "The three remaining having no other support than to firmly clutch the two number 10 wires and resting their feet on the shifting flooring of the platform."

They decided to send the cable car out in a rescue attempt, but were uncertain of whom to send. Judge Hulett wrote, "A young man named William Ellis stepped forward and said, 'I am your man.'"

A twelve-foot ladder was tied to the bottom of the basket and Ellis set out, with instructions to only bring back one man at a time because the engineers did not know how much strain the cable car could handle. However, Ellis abandoned these instructions and, upon the pleading of the stranded men not to be left behind, he decided to bring back all three. Judge Hulett wrote, "The basket, the capacity of which was but for two, was slowly drawn to shore, laden with four stalwart men and the four safely landed amid the shouts from the bystanders that silenced the raging elements."

# Bibliography

Ahrens, Edward W. *The Devil's Hole Massacre*. Sanborn, NY: Rissa Productions, 2004.

Barbuto, Richard V. *Niagara 1814: America Invades Canada*. Lawrence: University of Kansas Press, 2000.

Brown, Dee. *Bury My Heart at Wounded Knee*. New York: Holt Publishing Co., 1991.

Carroll, B.R., ed. *Historical Collection of South Carolina*. 2 vols. New York: Harper & Bros., 1936.

Clune, Henry W. *The Genesee*. Syracuse, NY: Syracuse University Press, 1890.

Cook, Lura Lincoln. *The War of 1812 on the Frontier*. Buffalo, NY: Buffalo & Erie County Historical Society, 1961.

Dunlap, Orrin E. *Unpublished Papers*. Niagara Falls Public Library Local History Department, 1946.

Duquemin, Colin K. *Niagara Rebels: The Niagara Frontier in the Upper Canada Rebellion*. St. Catharines, ON: Norman Enterprises, 2001.

Graymont, Barbara. *The Iroquois*. New York: Chelsea House Publishing, 1989.

Jennings, Francis. *The Founders of America*. New York: W.W. Norton & Company, 1993.

Lewis, Clarence O. *Collected Articles from the Niagara Falls Gazette*. Niagara Falls Public Library Local History Department, 1950.

Merrill, Arch. *Land of the Senecas*. Rochester, NY: Seneca Book Binding Co., 1958.

Porter, Peter A. *A Brief History of Old Fort Niagara*. Buffalo: The Mathews-Northrup Co., 1896.

Stranges, John B. *The Rainbow Never Fades*. New York: Peter Lang Publishing Co., 2007.

Turner, Orsamus. *Pioneer History of the Holland Purchase*. Buffalo, NY: George H. Derby & Company, 1850.

Williams, Edward T. *Collected Articles from the Niagara Falls Gazette*. Niagara Falls Public Library Local History Department, 1938.

Williams, Ted C. *The Reservation*. Syracuse, NY: Syracuse University Press, 1976.

# About the Author

Bob Kostoff is a native of Niagara Falls and was educated in local schools. He graduated summa cum laude from Niagara University. A retired journalist, he worked for the *Niagara Falls Gazette* in the Lockport Bureau, for the *Buffalo Courier-Express* and for the *Lockport Union-Sun & Journal*. While he covered all aspects of the western New York scene for the newspapers, he researched and wrote hundreds of feature articles on local history. He is the author of several other books, both fiction and nonfiction. He currently writes a local history column for the weekly newspaper, the *Niagara Falls Reporter*.

# ALSO AVAILABLE

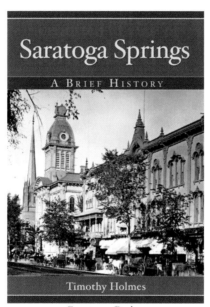

*Saratoga Springs*
by Timothy Holmes
978.1.59629.452.3 * 160 pp * $19.99

People from all walks of life came to Saratoga Springs to enjoy horse racing, gambling and other popular vices. But when the springs dried up and gambling was outlawed, the town's future was in dire peril. Find out how the town managed to avoid the slow death that might have overtaken it.

# YOU MIGHT ALSO ENJOY

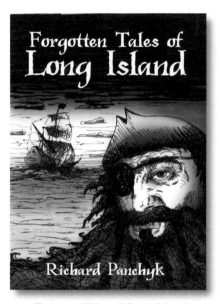

*Forgotten Tales of Long Island*
by Richard Panchyk
978.1.59629.381.6 * 160 pp * $14.99

R ichard Panchyk's new book will befuddle, baffle and bemuse even lifelong residents of Long Island. Culled from period newspapers, books and historical records, these brief tales cover everything from the price of Plum Island— a barrel of biscuits and a few fish hooks—to swamp serpents and cats riding horses.

Visit us at
www.historypress.net